A BATCHELOR'S DELIGHT

The Adventures of a Family Historian

Anne Batchelor

Arms granted to Daniel Bachiler of Aston Clinton and of the Privy Chamber in 1606.

(Brian Breton)

Highgate Publications (Beverley) Ltd.
1990

THIS BOOK IS DEDICATED TO
MY DEAR MOTHER AND FATHER
WHO GAVE ME THE GIFT OF LIFE
AND ALSO TO
DANIEL, EMILY AND THE REST OF MY BATCHELORS
WHOSE DISCOVERY HAS BROUGHT ME
SUCH DELIGHT

British Library Cataloguing in Publication Data

Batchelor, Anne
    A Batchelor's delight: the adventures of a family historian.
    1. England. Families. Genealogical aspects
    I. Title
    929.20942

ISBN 0-948929-40-5

Published by Highgate Publications (Beverley) Ltd.
24 Wylies Road, Beverley, HU17 7AP
Telephone (0482) 866826

Printed and Typeset in 10 on 11pt Plantin by
B.A. Press, 2-4 Newbegin, Lairgate, Beverley, HU17 8EG
Telephone (0482) 882232

Front Cover Picture
Reproduced by kind permission of Viscount De L'Isle, V.C., K.G.

Back Cover
Happy in a graveyard

Family History research is a quiet study of one's predecessors, who they were and what they did; perhaps the recovery of some document from the centuries' dust in which it has lain and from whose faded pages a man or woman steps forth without whom we ourselves would never have been. Discovering those documents and glimpsing, for an instant, those men and women has been my great delight. In the words of Sir John Harington, godson of Queen Elizabeth I, 'I write from wonder and affection.'

Contents

ANNE BATCHELOR'S FAMILY TREE

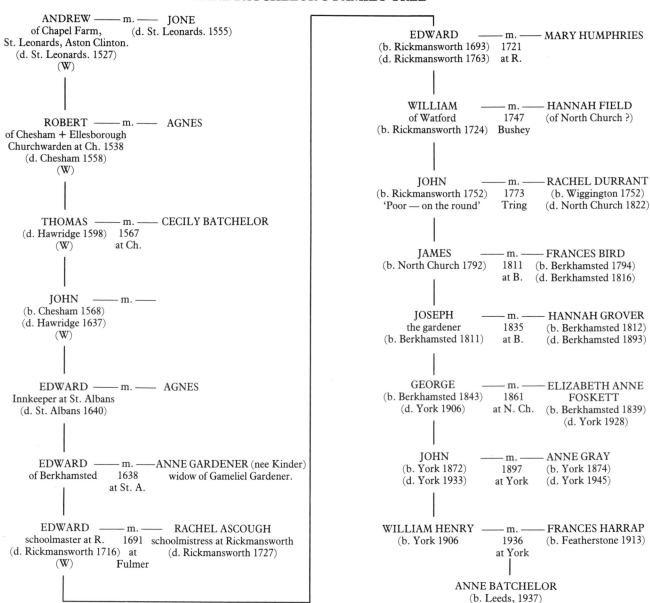

ANDREW —— m. —— JONE
of Chapel Farm,   (d. St. Leonards. 1555)
St. Leonards, Aston Clinton.
(d. St. Leonards. 1527)
(W)

ROBERT —— m. —— AGNES
of Chesham + Ellesborough
Churchwarden at Ch. 1538
(d. Chesham 1558)
(W)

THOMAS —— m. —— CECILY BATCHELOR
(d. Hawridge 1598)   1567
(W)   at Ch.

JOHN —— m. ——
(b. Chesham 1568)
(d. Hawridge 1637)
(W)

EDWARD —— m. —— AGNES
Innkeeper at St. Albans
(d. St. Albans 1640)

EDWARD —— m. —— ANNE GARDENER (nee Kinder)
of Berkhamsted   1638   widow of Gameliel Gardener.
at St. A.

EDWARD —— m. —— RACHEL ASCOUGH
schoolmaster at R.   1691   schoolmistress at Rickmansworth
(d. Rickmansworth 1716) at   (d. Rickmansworth 1727)
(W)   Fulmer

EDWARD —— m. —— MARY HUMPHRIES
(b. Rickmansworth 1693)   1721
(d. Rickmansworth 1763)   at R.

WILLIAM —— m. —— HANNAH FIELD
of Watford   1747   (of North Church ?)
(b. Rickmansworth 1724) Bushey

JOHN —— m. —— RACHEL DURRANT
(b. Rickmansworth 1752)   1773   (b. Wiggington 1752)
'Poor — on the round' Tring (d. North Church 1822)

JAMES —— m. —— FRANCES BIRD
(b. North Church 1792)   1811   (b. Berkhamsted 1794)
at B.   (d. Berkhamsted 1816)

JOSEPH —— m. —— HANNAH GROVER
the gardener   1835   (b. Berkhamsted 1812)
(b. Berkhamsted 1811) at B. (d. Berkhamsted 1893)

GEORGE —— m. —— ELIZABETH ANNE
(b. Berkhamsted 1843)   1861   FOSKETT
(d. York 1906)   at N. Ch.   (b. Berkhamsted 1839)
(d. York 1928)

JOHN —— m. —— ANNE GRAY
(b. York 1872)   1897   (b. York 1874)
(d. York 1933)   at York   (d. York 1945)

WILLIAM HENRY —— m. —— FRANCES HARRAP
(b. York 1906   1936   (b. Featherstone 1913)
at York

ANNE BATCHELOR
(b. Leeds, 1937)

W = Will   iv

Foreword

Research into family history is becoming increasingly popular. When Anne Batchelor sent details of her research to the B.B.C.'s monthly history programme, *Timewatch*, the editor realised that he was on to something rather special. I was the producer sent off to meet her to explore the possibility of a film.

Working with Anne to make a documentary about family history was one of the most enjoyable experiences of my professional life. It is also very instructive for a T.V. producer to see, from the other side, what it feels like to be descended upon by a B.B.C. film crew. While I learned, with increasing respect, about how she had done her research, she was learning a great deal faster how best to present her ideas on television.

This book, written with the same humour and talent that she brought to the film, is a wonderful tale of scholarship and enthusiasm which will be read with great enjoyment by those who have already embarked on the adventure of tracing their family's history. It will, without doubt, inspire others to begin *their* journey into the past.

Antonia Benedek
B.B.C. Television Producer

Part of Chapel Farm in Buckinghamshire.

Introduction

I stood in an old overgrown churchyard in York and tossed a flower into a tangle of brambles and weeds which covered the grave of a man who was employed at the nearby Gas Works and who died in 1890. I stood in a derelict churchyard in Kent and gently placed a single red rose on an ivy-covered tomb in memory of a Groom of the Privy Chamber to Anne of Denmark, who died in 1618/19.

Between those two events lay four years of obsessive family research and an amazing adventure of discovery which led me from my high-rise home in Yorkshire to the Record Offices of the south, from churches and farmhouses in out-of-the-way villages to the claustrophobic, overcrowded London Underground, until one day I found myself in front of a television camera in a beautiful stately home in Kent. I remember thinking to myself, 'Is this really happening to me? How did I get myself into this?'

Many years before, I had watched the television version of Alex Haley's story of his search for his African *Roots*. I remember vividly the sequence which showed the moment when he finally stood in the African village from which, he believed, his ancestor, Kunta Kinte, had been snatched away by slavers. I felt a shiver of excitement when the old village storyteller, who held in his head all the history of the tribe, told the gathered villagers, 'Once upon a time, Kunta Kinte, a boy from this village, went into the forest and never came back.'

I remember thinking how wonderful it would be if, one day, I could stand where *my* ancestors had been. Perhaps I could knock at someone's door and ask, 'May I take a photograph of your house? My great-grandfather once lived here'. Well, I never did that, for my great-grandfather's house no longer exists, but I did knock on the door of a timbered farmhouse in

— a habit of swearing at the postman if he brings no mail,

— an aversion to wasting time on such things as housework and meals,

— the constant urge to visit obscure villages no-one has ever heard of,

— a tendency to talk to oneself, muttering meaningless comments such as, '— but he couldn't have married Eliza. He died before she was born.'

The strangest aspect of this malady is that, the worse the illness becomes, the more the patient seems to enjoy it. My friends ask me, 'Whatever will you do when you finish your research?' There really is no answer to that, for each new discovery reveals yet more mysteries to be solved. It is a quest without an end.

My high-rise home in Leeds.

Buckinghamshire and ask permission to take a photograph '— because my 13xgreat-grandfather, Andrew Bacheler, died here in 1527'!

Family research has been described as an obsessive illness for which there is no cure. The symptoms are as follows:

— a glazed expression and a far-away look in the eye,

— an obsession with writing letters to perfect strangers,

Chapter One

A Flower for Theophilus

'To begin at the beginning — '
Dylan Thomas.

'Have you found any villains — or anyone famous?' I have lost count of the number of times I have been asked that by curious friends who don't realise the satisfaction of finding simple farmworkers and housewives if they are your own blood and bone. Sadly I appear to have no villains in my family — no great scandal or skeletons in the cupboard. I say 'sadly' because such people add colour to a family's story. However, I did find someone famous, quite by accident, but more of him in a later chapter. To begin at the beginning:

Initially I knew very little about my distant family, but I had been able to gather a considerable amount of information about my parents' early days from our conversations together. My mother, Frances, when she was only a tiny mite of four, lost her mother in an outbreak of influenza in 1917. Because her father was a miner, working long hours in the pit at Featherstone, he was unable to care for his baby son and little daughter. Reluctantly he had to let them both go into children's homes. My mother has told me many a story about those years. When she grew up she went into service, living in an 'Upstairs, Downstairs' world where she made her way from 'tweeny' to cook and then, moving upstairs, to Nanny. One day I would like to tell her story, but so far the research of my Batchelor ancestors has filled my days.

I knew that my father had been born in Railway Street, York, in 1906 and grew up in Rougier Street, just around the corner from the 15th-century house where his mother, Anne Gray, had been born. He worked in the old-established firm of Rowntrees, in the cellars of the elegant hotel beside the railway station, and in many other jobs before moving to Leeds to drive for 41 years for Schweppes. This is where all family research begins — with what we already know. From that we move into the unknown.

The first step on my ancestral journey was taken when Grandma Batchelor's family Bible came into my hands. I was visiting my Aunt Annie at her home in Rowntree Avenue, a street heavy with the smell of warm, melted chocolate. What a pity that it has been necessary, for environmental reasons, to banish that smell from the streets around the factory. As a child I had revelled in the smell every time I stepped off the bus in Burdyke Avenue. Perhaps my great love of chocolate stems from those formative years!

In Aunt Annie's garden were my cousin's small daughters, playing with a large, battered book. This proved to be the Batchelor family Bible and I was delighted to see my father's name on the beautifully illustrated page of Children's Births. There it was: 'William Henry Batchelor — 5 November 1906'. My aunt said, half jokingly, that I could have the Bible if I could manage to carry it back to Leeds. It was huge and heavy, with great metal clasps, but I still remember the delight with which I staggered away with it clasped to my bosom. Full of anticipation I travelled home on the bus with it heavy on my knee.

When I got it home and studied it in greater detail I found, to my great surprise, the names of two children I could not identify. There were Uncle George and Aunt Annie; there, too, were Uncle Fred, Aunt Zillah and my father, William Henry, but who on earth were James Alfred Batchelor and Mary Batchelor? I had no Uncle James nor an Aunt Mary. My father, too, was mystified. He had never heard of either of them. Turning the page to the one headed 'Deaths', all was revealed. Baby James Alfred, born 28 May 1900, had only lived until 24 October. Little Mary, born 6 July 1908, had died on 15 May 1910, before her second birthday.

So here was my first experience of the mysteries thrown up by family research which turn us all into

My mother as a child.

My father, William Henry Batchelor, as a young man.

2

The Batchelor family c.1916, my father centre, front row.

demented Miss Marples or Sherlock Holmeses. I was now gripped by an insatiable curiosity to know more about my Batchelors, but I had no idea where to begin. I knew that both my father and grandfather came from York and, as far as I knew, York would hold the whole story of my family. At this point I remember receiving an interesting 'phone call from a lady who said that she was researching the Batchelors of Hertfordshire. She had found me in the Leeds 'phone book and wondered whether that was *my* family. 'Oh, no,' I said with great conviction. 'We are a Yorkshire family.' I rang off without asking her name and number. I could kick myself now, for we are probably both researching the same family. Perhaps she will read my book and get in touch again. Who knows? I remember thinking to myself, 'Thank goodness I don't have to travel to Hertfordshire to research *my* family. Just twenty miles to York and I'm back to my roots.' How wrong I was.

On a visit to Uncle Fred shortly before he died I told him of my interest in the family. 'Have you ever seen your grandfather's birth certificate and marriage lines?' he asked. 'Here they are.' He produced two wonderful, crumbling yellow documents which I took with eager hands. 'Did you know,' he asked, 'that your great-grandmother was Eliza Foskett and she came from Luton, where they made straw hats?' This mention of Luton was to prove a red herring, but at this early stage I was so green that I would believe anything anyone told me. I know now that any family information not backed up by concrete evidence such as a certificate should be taken with an enormous pinch of salt. I remember hearing of a gentleman who was very proud of the family tradition that they were descended from the Duke of Wellington, until he discovered, to his great disappointment, that his great-grandfather kept a public house called The Duke of Wellington.

My grandfather's birth certificate gave me the names of his parents, George and Elizabeth Ann Batchelor (née Foskett) and an address. Two books from a jumble sale explained the next step. They told me of census returns, and I made the happy discovery that the Leeds Reference Library held these, on microfilm, for the whole of Yorkshire. I went hot-foot to see them. At the library I was inducted into the mysteries of using 'a reader'. To me, a reader suggests a person, but this reader proved to be an antiquated contraption like an overgrown TV set with a large screen whose dim grey light was to reveal the next step in my quest. This would take me, in one giant leap, out of Yorkshire and into the unknown.

I studied the census return for Paver Lane, York, as this was the address on my grandfather's birth certificate. To my great dismay George and Eliza were not there in either 1871 (the year before my grandfather's birth) or 1881 (when he would have been a little lad of nine). However, there was a Batchel*der* family there. At first I was put off by the strange spelling, but I have since discovered 30 different spellings of proven members of my family. This is because, for many centuries, spelling was phonetic. The Batchelders I found in Paver Lane were Theophilus, his wife Mary and his children Thomas Baker Batchelder and Elizabeth.

No one in my family had ever heard of Theophilus, who was described in the census as a gas fitter from Berkhamsted in Hertfordshire. Reading his name aloud, with the stress on '*der*' you can actually hear his Herts. accent, which is rather nice. Going to my road atlas, which was to prove one of my most valuable aids on my genealogical quest over the next few years, I found Berkhamsted, about ten miles from Luton, where Uncle Fred had said my great-grandmother, Eliza, had originated. Here I made my first glaring error. I guessed that Theophilus must have been the father of my great-grandfather George. I boasted to all my friends about my great-great-grandfather with the posh name. In fact he proved to be George's second cousin. He was the first of my Berkhamstead Batchelors to be lured to the industrial north by the high wages in the factories of York.

Now I wanted to see Paver Lane for myself, along with the other streets where my family had lived. I had a great desire, too, to find the place where George and Eliza, Theophilus and his Mary, were buried. The helpful young lady at York Reference Library found an old map of York showing Paver Lane, beside St. Margaret's Church, Walmgate. 'I'm afraid all that area has been demolished,' she said, 'but perhaps you can still see where the lane used to be.' She also introduced me to the International Genealogical Index, or I.G.I.

My parents on their wedding day.

This is an amazing index of baptisms and marriages, nationwide, compiled by the Mormon Church for their own use but generously made available to all researchers, free of charge, at many libraries and Record Offices. There I saw recorded the baptism of Theophilus Batchelder's two children at St. Margaret's, Walmgate, in the city of York. Finding him on the I.G.I. somehow made him become more real. The librarian then found some old photographs of Redness Street, where I had discovered that both George and Eliza had died. Librarians such as this are the unsung heroes of genealogical research. So many men and women like her have gone out of their way to help people like me as we take our first halting steps through the bewildering amount of archive material which survives. Bless them, we would make little progress without their interest and helpfulness.

So I set off to find the lost Paver Lane and the last resting place of my York family. This was my first visit to a Batchelor site. It was an eerie feeling to walk along what survived of Paver Lane. All the houses were gone. Only a small brick building with a hay-loft remained, but to my intense delight the paving stones on which my George and Eliza and Theophilus had walked were still there. I felt like Alex Haley must have felt when he stood at last in his African village. It was a feeling I was to experience many times in my genealogical adventure. As I stood there, savouring the moment, I couldn't help thinking that Paver Lane could not have been a very pleasant place to live. The lane was extremely narrow, which would have made the houses very dark. There was no running water, for a communal pump in a yard was marked on the old street map.

Its one redeeming feature was the fact that Paver Lane backed on to the churchyard of St. Margaret's. In 1849 the records of St. Margaret's note: 'One young sycamore tree and twenty-three lime trees planted', and the writer comments, 'These trees are of no value except for ornament.' This grassy 'God's acre', with its trees and singing birds, must have provided an oasis of

No. of Schedule	ROAD, STREET, &c., and No. or NAME of HOUSE	HOUSES		NAME and Surname of each Person	RELATION to Head of Family	CONDITION as to Marriage	AGE last Birthday		Rank, Profession, or OCCUPATION	WHERE BORN	
7	7 James Street	1		George Batchelor	Head	Mar	38		Glass Blower	Northchurch Herts	
				Eliza A. Batchelor	Wife	Mar		42		Birkhampstead Herts	
				Thomas Batchelor	Son	Unm	18		Labourer	Northchurch Herts	
				Stephen H. Batchelor	Son	Unm	16		Do	Do	
				Joseph W. Batchelor	Son		12		Scholar	Birkhampstead Herts	
				John Batchelor	Son		9		Scholar	City of York	
				James A. Batchelor	Son		6		Scholar	Do Do	
				Rose H. Batchelor	daur			4		Do Do	
				Eliza E. Batchelor	daur			2		Do Do	

1881 Census, York, showing my great grandparents with their family.

green in an area packed with dingy, overcrowded houses. Judging by the burial registers of Saint Margaret's it was a most unhealthy place in which to live. Many adults died of bronchitis or dysentery, and the records show a sorrowful procession of dead babies carried off by sickness and convulsions. As their family increased in number my great-grandparents moved to James Street and, later to Redness Street. These were both wider streets and obviously a great improvement on Paver Lane, but I often wonder whether my Batchelors ever regretted their migration to the big city whose streets were hardly paved with gold.

Now to find their last resting place. I wrote to the kind lady at the York Reference Library, who told me that burial records were kept on microfilm at the York City Archives. This proved to be one of those small, silent, slightly dusty offices with which I was to become so familiar over the next few years. I was welcomed by the Archivist, to whom I poured out my family story. I imagine she has to deal with a steady stream of people such as myself, eaten up by an insatiable curiosity about their ancestors, but having little idea of how to use an archive office.

She put me in front of a reader. 'Oh, yes,' I said with great confidence, 'I know how to use one of these,' and proceeded to put the film on upside down and back to front. Patiently she unravelled the film and set me going again, this time the right way up. I had no idea when my York ancestors had died, so finding them was a long and tedious task. However, the tedium of the search makes the delight of discovery all the more intense. If it were too easy there would be little thrill. I dread the day when we can find our ancestors by merely pressing a button on a computer instead of being able to toil over the records for ourselves. I twirled my way happily through years and years of deceased inhabitants of York until, at last, to my great satisfaction, I found:

BATCHELOR, Theophilus. Buried Jan. 7th 1890. Age 69
Occupation — labourer. Address — Albert Street, Walmgate
Cause of death — Cancer.

BATCHELOR, George. Buried March 2nd 1906. Age 63

With my parents.

Occupation — Gas stoker. Address — 27 Redness Street.

Cause of death — Cancer.

BATCHELOR, Eliza Ann. Buried June 6th 1928. Age 89

Occupation — widow. Address — 14 Redness Street.

BATCHELOR, John. Buried December 5th 1933. Age 61

Occupation — Railway engine driver. Address — 4 Rougier Street.

Cause of death — Cardiac disease.

Theophilus, George and Eliza were all buried in the old York Cemetery, on the aptly named Cemetery Road, while my grandfather, John, with his wife, Anne, was in the modern cemetery at Fulford. Armed with plans of both cemeteries I went to look for them.

My grandparents' grave in the modern cemetery was easy to find but I was sad to see that their stone was badly weathered and discoloured. I left some flowers there and made up my mind that, one day, I would have the stone restored. A few years later, at a meeting of the Friends of York Cemetery, I was approached by a gentleman who told me that he had worked with my grandfather's brother, Alf, in the stoneyard many years ago. He would be very pleased to restore the stone for me. He did a wonderful job and John and Anne's last resting place is now clearly marked.

The old cemetery was a different kettle of fish. Here

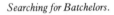

Searching for Batchelors.

I should warn the budding genealogist to beware of helpful local inhabitants who tell you that the place you seek is 'just five minutes up this road'. Five minutes, perhaps, if your name is Sebastian Coe! For us lesser mortals it is more likely to be 25. At last, footsore and weary, I reached my goal. The cemetery was vast and, in many places, overgrown. It was a place of singing birds, wild flowers and numerous butterflies. With mounting excitement, map clutched in my hand, I counted my way across the many interlacing paths until I found Eliza's plot. Alas, it was knee-high with grass and nettles. There was nothing to show who was buried there. The graves of George and old Theophilus, too, were submerged under a heap of brambles and weeds. I put a few flowers among Eliza's nettles and on George's plot, too. Sadly, I couldn't get near to the

Birthplace of my grandmother, Annie Gray.

grave of old Theophilus for brambles, but I tossed one flower into them, whispering very quietly under my breath, 'There Theophilus, I promised I would come.' After all, I didn't want people to hear me and think I was odd, talking to a man who had been dead for almost a hundred years. At that moment he seemed very real to me.

Over the next few years I was to ramble round many a cemetery and churchyard seeking the last resting places of my ancestors, but for me there will always be something very special about that first one. I was somehow in the presence of George and Eliza and Theophilus. For the first time I felt that they were not mere names on a chart but real people. For me this is the magic of family research. They become 'my Emily', 'my Daniel', 'my Eliza'. There is a sense in which, by remembering our ancestors, we restore them to life for a moment.

I well remember my first visit to the Wills Room at the Public Record Office in London and my shock at seeing the testators listed as 'the deceased'. Though my head knows that my Batchelors are long dead, my heart seems to see them still living their lives in their own time, almost within reach. It is curious that other family historians have told me of the same feeling. We comb through musty old documents for a name and, on finding it, we say not, 'There it is,' but *'There* you are, Emily. Gotcha!' As one schoolgirl, pouring over Electoral Registers, said to me with shining eyes, 'Look Miss, look! Here is my grand-dad!' I suppose it is a confirmation of my belief as a Christian that when the body dies the individual does not cease to exist. Confucius once said that to serve those now dead as if they were living is the highest achievement of true filial piety. I like to think that George and Eliza, along with all my other ancestors, are aware of my desire to know all about them, and are aware, too, of the affection I feel for them.

This affection results, I think, from the realisation that I owe my very existence not only to my beloved parents but to George and Eliza, too. Had they not met, married and produced my grandfather, then my own father would never have been born and I would not be here. It is a curious feeling which ties me to my ancestors with bonds of gratitude. Even old Theophilus played a part in my existence. Had he not come to York in the 1840s and encouraged great-grandfather George to bring his family here, then my father would probably have been born in Hertfordshire and would never have met my mother. I probably would have been born as a result of his marriage to a Hertfordshire girl, but I would not be me, for the Harrap and Godber genes inherited from my mother's family would not be part of me.

So it was I took my first halting steps on my genealogical journey of discovery. It was to be a real adventure. I would make many new friends, learn new skills, suffer great frustration, find myself in the strangest of situations and, above all, have great fun.

Duggie, my postie.

Return to my roots at Chapel Farm.   © *Antonia Benedek*

8

Chapter Two

Trips to the Treasure-House

*'Every journey an adventure, every library a
treasure-house'*

John Unett.

I gave a muffled gasp of delight. The gentleman sitting next to me turned and whispered, 'Have you found something?' 'Yes,' I said. 'I've found the marriage of my great-grandparents,' and then, with great pride, 'I came all the way from Yorkshire to find this.' 'Have you?' he said. 'I came all the way from Australia to find my family.'

Thus, in the Hertford Record Office, I was introduced to the obsession which drives family historians to go to any lengths to find their ancestors. The Australian's search took him to the other side of the world where, that morning, he found a newspaper account of the trial of his convict ancestor for burglary. My search had not taken me so far but I was equally delighted to find my George and Eliza.

I had not realised, when I began the search for my family, how many miles I was to travel or what strange and thrilling places I would visit. I had foolishly imagined that a quick run up the A64 to York in my faithful old Reliant Robin would bring me to the source of all my family information in less than half an hour. Instead, I was to became a regular visitor at my local travel agent and the despair of their extremely helpful and efficient staff. I'm sure they cringed whenever they saw me approach their counter. They came to expect a request for travel details to some obscure town or village no one had ever heard of. As Frances once remarked plaintively, 'Wouldn't you rather go to New York? It's far easier to get you there than to Rickmansworth, wherever that is.'

It was at this point that I began to make regular use of my local taxi-lady, Audrey. She has bravely faced my 5.30 a.m. bookings in the depths of winter as well as on lovely summer mornings. Together we have shivered our way to the Wellington Street Coach Station for the first Rapide coach south. Each time I have had to give her the latest development of my family quest, for she now feels part of the adventure. A vital part she is, too, for in all the five years of my research she has never let me down. True, there was one nasty winter's morning when her alarm clock failed and she woke with a start to the realisation that my coach departed in a little over 20 minutes. Throwing her clothes over her nightwear and pulling on a woolly hat, she rushed round for me and we arrived at the coach station as they were loading up. It was a near thing — but we made it and Audrey's fine record was untarnished. Her enthusiasm and encouragement have added greatly to the enjoyment of my adventures.

Many things cross my mind as I stand waiting for Audrey. As I look around me at all the closed curtains where all the sensible people are asleep in bed, I think to myself, 'I must be *mad*, getting up at this time of the morning.' Then I become aware of what a lovely time the early morning is and how sad that most of the time we sleep through it. To stand in the stillness of a January morning and study the stars overhead is a wonderfully calming experience. Even in springtime it is still dark at 5.15 a.m. but the first birds are singing and I have the distinct impression that I am their sole audience and that they are singing for me alone. Of course, I know that this is not really true. They are simply rehearsing for their time of courtship. Still, it's a nice thought and I can be excused, at that time of morning, if I am not strictly rational in my thoughts. The overwhelming feeling, however, as I wait, is a breathless anticipation, for I have no idea what new genealogical treasures I shall unearth when I reach my destination.

Wellington Street at 6 a.m. is not the most salubrious place to wait for a coach. A little before the hour an official arrives to unlock the waiting room. He wakes up the old vagrant sleeping on the wooden seat outside and hoses the seat down so that it is fit for passengers to sit on. Then the Rapide coach arrives, luggage is stowed in the rear and the journey begins. I try desperately to stay awake until we reach the motorway, when the hostess brings round the hot drinks which are so welcome on a cold morning. Then I slip into a deep sleep, only waking when we turn off the motorway. I think that the sudden change of direction and different tone of the coach engine must reach deep down into my subconscious and rouse me.

I look forward to my snooze on the coach. Having to be up at 3.30 a.m., with the help of no fewer than *three* alarm clocks all set at slightly different times, I am ready to put my head back, settle into my comfy seat and blot out. What bliss! However, there have been times when I have been seated next to someone who wanted to carry on a conversation all the 200 miles to London. I have to say that, being a sociable person, I have always enjoyed these conversations but regret them later when my eyes start to glaze over in the early afternoon. Over the years my travelling companions have been most interesting company. On one occasion I found myself sitting next to a member of the House of Lords. He told me that he went to London by coach

Berkhamsted High Street as George and Eliza would have known it.

every Monday and returned to Leeds at the end of the week, again by coach. He had had a fascinating career and was an entertaining raconteur, so the journey passed very quickly. When we parted company at Victoria Coach Station he invited me to visit him at the House of Lords if ever I wanted a conducted tour. Sadly I never seem to have found the time to take up his kind invitation.

Another time I sat beside a young girl who was going to London to meet Esther Rantzen. This was in the early days of Childline. She had a harrowing story to tell of abuse in her own home, but had managed to come to terms with the experience. Now she was anxious to make her story public in the hope of helping other children in the same situation. Then I met a lady who was going to Saudi Arabia to be nanny to the children of a wealthy family. On another journey I sat beside a fine young man who was doing voluntary work with severely retarded children. So the list goes on. My friends often question my solitary journeys, but one of the great advantages of travelling alone is that you are more inclined to strike up conversation with a stranger, and it does help to while away the time. Far more enlightening than snoring all the way to Victoria!

On the first of these genealogical journeys I made my way from Victoria to Moorgate Underground Station, where I remembered with a shudder the dreadful Tube disaster many years ago in which so many had died and where also great heroism and bravery made the headlines. Moorgate to Hertford was an easy journey and I soon found myself at the Salisbury Arms where I had booked a room for a couple of nights. This was a fine old building, timbered and decorated with pargeting. It seemed a typical old English inn. It was with great surprise, therefore, that I took my dinner that evening in the dining room which was also a Chinese restaurant. As I munched my way through my delicious Chinese chicken, I pondered on the adventure which was now unfolding. What would I discover at the Hertford Record Office in the morning? Would I find the marriage of my George and Eliza?

What would I learn about old Theophilus? How far back into the past would I be able to reach? With my head buzzing with all these questions I went early to bed, to recover from my 3.30 a.m. start in Leeds.

In the morning, surprisingly bright and early, I made my way past the stone hart on the War Memorial, ('Morning, deer!' I muttered) and up the long hill to the County Hall which housed the Record Office. Of course, being so keen, I arrived before the doors were opened. It was a lovely autumn morning. It had rained heavily overnight and there was a chill dampness in the air, but a misty golden light filtered through the trees. I took a few moments to enjoy the stillness — a habit I developed during thirty years of teaching in overcrowded classrooms. A quiet moment snatched before the start of a busy day can help you cope with all the hard work and frustration the day may bring.

Suddenly there was a rattle of keys and the door of the 'treasure-house' swung open to me. With mounting excitement I entered. I was met by a strange, musty smell with which I would soon become familiar. It was the odour of old parchment, brittle yellow paper and dust. The faintest whiff of that smell now makes the heart beat faster with anticipation. I found myself in an entrance hall with a staircase to the left and a door on my right. Taking the easy option I went through the door and found myself in the Herts. Local Studies Library. I was greeted by a smiling lady who was to become a good friend over the next few years. Shelagh Head asked me to sign in and then wanted to know how she could help. I told her my quest and asked about the Berkhamsted census of 1871, which might show my George and Eliza with their family before they moved north to York. Shelagh initiated me into the mysteries of her electronically operated reader which obviates the tedious wheel-churning when winding the microfilm. We spent a hilarious few minutes as I learnt how *not* to use it. With the control wheel turned too far either way, the film flew past so quickly that I found myself in another village altogether. The machine needed a gentle touch and a quick use of the brake, or I would find myself seesawing between villages in a manner guaranteed to bring on an attack of vertigo.

At last I tamed the reader and was able to wander through the streets of Berkhamsted in the year 1871. This is real time-travelling. I could scarcely believe my eyes when I found George and Eliza so easily. I had spent months poring over the census returns for the vast city of York, looking for them. Here, in a small town, it took no time at all. There they were, living in the aptly named George Street:

George Batchelor — aged 27 — Labourer

Eliza Ann Batchelor — aged 30 — Straw plaiter

Henry — son — aged 6

Mary Ann — daughter — aged 4

Joseph — son — aged 2

Of course my grandfather, John, was not there for he was born in York the following year, but it was a lovely feeling to be able to see my family in residence in their own village. Shelagh showed me how to use this incredibly clever reader to take a photocopy of the entry so that I could take it home with me. She then brought me a cup of coffee to calm me down. After this brief pause I was off again. Up the stairs I went, in pursuit of Parish Registers, to the Herts. Record Office.

Again I signed in, marvelling at the number of previous signatures which were followed by the words, 'Family History'. At last I was in the company of like-minded people. I gazed around me. The walls were lined with books, catalogues and filing-cabinets. A treasure-house indeed! Almost every seat in the room was taken. Some researchers were using the now familiar readers and churning away at their handles. No incredible electronic gadgetry here. The readers were all people-powered. Other folk were leaning over enormous maps or picking their way through exciting-looking boxes of parchment. I told my story to a patient young assistant and asked for the marriage register of Luton. Had not my Uncle Fred told me that Eliza came from Luton, 'where they made straw hats'? No doubt the marriage took place in the bride's parish.

I was shown the system for finding registers, which were mostly on film. Unfortunately every Record Office seems to have a system unique to itself, so it is always a challenge on a first visit to see how soon I can crack the system. However, there was an unforeseen snag. I had not realised that Luton is in Bedfordshire and not in Herts. The Luton register was at Bedford, 30 miles away. What frustration! 'Never mind,' said my helpful young lady. 'If the groom was from Berkhamsted then the banns would have been called at *his* church as well as at Luton. We do have the Berkhamsted banns book.'

After a surprisingly short wait, during which I wandered along the bookcases and found a section of useful books on my area, my banns book arrived. I took it to my place and, hands trembling with excitement, opened it at random. What a surprise! There was a John Thomas Batchelor, then a Peter James Batchelor — every entry on that page recorded the marriage of a Batchelor. I turned the pages. Still more Batchelors. I couldn't believe my eyes. Every marriage in that book seemed to have a groom who was a Batchelor. Then the penny dropped. Here was not a village full of matrimonially inclined Batchelors, but a village with a parish clerk who couldn't spell, '*Bachelor* of this parish'.

On the census I had seen that Eliza's first child had been born about 1864, so I started to look for the banns of their wedding that year and then worked backwards through the years. To my intense disappointment they were not there. With a glum face I returned the banns book to the assistant. 'No luck?' she asked. 'Then perhaps they married at North Church. It is the next village, almost adjoining Berkhamsted. You never know.' Indeed you don't. I found them easily in the North Church book. It was at this point that I gave my muffled gasp of delight which caught the attention of my Australian family historian. It was so good to share this special moment with someone who could understand my excitement.

To my great surprise the entry revealed that Eliza was not 'of Luton', as Uncle Fred had said, but of North Church, as was her bridegroom. The census had told me that she plaited straw for the hat trade and it was the half-remembered family reference to straw hats that had misled Uncle Fred into placing Eliza at Luton. Now I was able to get out the film of the North Church registers and see the entry of George and Eliza's marriage. Another surprise awaited me. Their marriage was solemnized on 1 December 1861, when George would have been 18-years-old and Eliza 22. However, they both gave their ages as 20. I was learning to treat with caution even official documents such as church registers.

Now came another shock. Under the column headed, 'Father's name and surname', I expected to find old Theophilus. Instead there was a Joseph Batchelor, a gardener. Reluctantly I had to reject my earlier theory that Theophilus was my 2xgreat-grandfather, but what a good thing that I had made that mistake in the first place. I would never have dreamt of Berkhamsted roots for my family had I not discovered Theophilus of Berkhamsted living in Paver Lane in York. Claiming him as my ancestor had been a glaring error, but it was a fortunate mistake for it led me south to Hertfordshire where I was to discover my real roots.

At this point my energy was flagging and I resorted to the County Hall restaurant, a beautiful spacious room where I bought an enormous salad and sat by the window overlooking the lawns. It takes some time for the eyes to re-focus after a morning on the readers, but I always begrudge the necessity of meal breaks. They are an unwelcome interruption I could well do without. Eating seems such a waste of precious time.

The afternoon found me combing the North Church register for George's birth. There he was:

'George — 2nd son of Joseph and Hannah Batcheldor
Born 14 Sept. 1843, Baptised 15 Oct. 1843'

Again Joseph was given as a gardener, so I knew I had the right family. Now I had the name of Joseph's wife, my 2x-great-grandmother Hannah. To find her full name I searched the North Church register for their marriage, but in vain. However, I was now learning the method of tracking down an ancestor. If not in their own parish — try next door. Sure enough, along the High Street to Berkhamsted and there they were.

'At St. Peter's, Berkhamstead — 30 November 1835
Joseph Batcheldor of this Parish — Bachelor
and Hannah Grover of this Parish — Spinster
were married in this church by Banns
by me James C. Browne   Curate'

Confirmation that this was *my* Joseph and Hannah came from the signature of the witness, William Foskett, father of my great-grandmother Eliza of the straw hats.

That was enough excitement for one day, so it was down the hill to the Salisbury Arms. I sat in the Chinese restaurant, stunned and boggle-eyed after the concentration of that first day's research. As I waited to be served, I took out my notebook and read through the day's discoveries. I have since noticed a distinct concern among waiters whenever I do this. Perhaps they think that I am a spy for Egon Ronay! I certainly get more attentive service after I take out my little book.

After a good night's sleep I was on the doorstep of the Record Office at opening time. Today time was short, for I had to get back to London in the afternoon to catch the evening coach home to Yorkshire. Hot on the trail now, I churned my way through films of the North Church and Berkhamsted registers to find the rest of Joseph and Hannah's family. Joseph's baptism was there, too. He was the first son of James and Frances Bachelor, born on 17 July 1811.

When I looked for the marriage of James and Frances I was in for a shock. They married on 15 July 1811, just two days before the birth of little Joseph. Then I noticed something curious. The witnesses at their wedding, Jos. Nightingale and Sarah Rouse, had married on the same day. Two days before the marriage of my James and his Frances Bird, an Edith Bachelor had married a Thomas Bird. Their witnesses were Mary Bird and John Glenister, who had just been married earlier the same day with Edith Bachelor as *their* witness. What a strange cluster of marriage and intermarriage. I wondered what the explanation might be.

Later a friend pointed out to me that 1811 was the time of the Napoleonic Wars. Perhaps James, Jos., Thomas and John were going away to war and decided to marry before they went, as many young couples did during the last war. Perhaps the vicar said, rather sharply, to James, 'You can't go away and leave poor Frances in that condition.' Or perhaps James had returned from serving in the Militia to be met by his anxious sweetheart, greatly increased in girth since he last saw her: 'James, I have something to tell you. I think we should go and see the vicar.'

However it was, Frances bore her son and reared him successfully. She had two more children, both girls, and then died at the pitifully early age of 22. When I discovered this I had a strange thought. If her only little boy, Joseph, had been sickly and died, I would never have existed. At that point in our family history all the future generations hung on the slender thread of the life of that one tiny baby. Knowing how often children died in infancy in those days, it seemed to me a small miracle that Frances did not lose her first baby. Then where would I be?

Now I became greedy for more of my family. I spent all that morning and early afternoon trawling in more Batchelors from the registers, not even taking time off for lunch. After all, I must get my priorities right. I had a quiet smile to myself when I found reference to a 'Charity for the Relief of Poor Bachelors' at Hemel Hempsted. I sometimes feel I could do with some financial help myself! Many people believe that family records survive only if the family is well-to-do but the reverse is nearer the truth. The poorer the family, the more likely they are to be living 'on the Parish' and, therefore, to be listed in parish records. The North Church records show that my Batchelors received clothing and money for medical help from the parish Overseers of the Poor:

'April 19 1795 Paid for a hat for Batchelder, 2d. 0d.
Paid for cloaths & shoes for — Dᵒ — 18s. 9d.
Nov 6, 1798 Paid Batchelor Casualty Poor, 6s. 0d.
Jan. 1801 Paid John Batchelor his wife ill, 2s. 6d.
Dec. 1801 ½cwt. Faggots for Batchelor's wife.'

John Batchelor was put on the round, an excellent system whereby an out-of-work man was given one day's work at each of several farms in the area. This would cost each farmer only one day's wage but would provide the labourer with an income which prevented him from being too much of a liability to the parish.

Quarter Sessions Records, too, are fascinating. Alice Crowche of Tring was indicted for petty larceny on 6 Feb. 1576. She stole '2 skeins of linen yarn from Richard Bachelor of Tring, husbandman'. Poor Alice, I wonder what her punishment would be? Justice was harsh in those days. Consider the fate of Ann Askew of Smithfield. She was burnt, the charge against her being 'favouring the reformation'. She would not implicate her friends. Her limbs had been previously dislocated by the rack. Poor brave Ann. The records for 1678 show Sir George Longe, Knt., of Cheping Wiccomb and John Batchelor of Amersham up before the magistrate 'for assaulting Frances, wife of Nathaniel Price'. What story lies behind that case, I wonder? I am constantly led astray by interesting entries which have nothing at all to do with my own research. How can I resist such snippets as, 'John Larradd of St. Giles, London, for assaulting Isabel Bond, widow, that he inhumanly and cruelly did pull and draw her by the hairs of her head wrapped about his right arm'? That sounds painful. And what about 'Paid Austin for his trouble with Mary Witman, 2s. 6d.'?

I have made many return visits to Hertford and have always blessed the staff there for their patience and helpfulness when I was so new and green and ignorant. Shelagh has now retired from her Local Studies Library, taking with her the collection of cat photographs which were so much a feature of her library. However, it is to her that I owe my greatest debt of gratitude. One day, when I had been researching for over a year, a lady from Bedfordshire signed in at Shelagh's desk, entering 'Family History' as the subject of her research. Shelagh asked, 'Which family?' and Mary Geary replied 'I'm researching my mother's family. They were Batchelors,' 'Oh,' said Shelagh, 'We have a Miss Batchelor who comes down from Yorkshire. Would you like her address?' Thus Shelagh put me in touch with the lady who was to become like a sister to me.

My first meeting with Mary was an odd sensation. We had corresponded for about a year, swapping Batchelor information and sharing our successes and frustrations, so that we felt that we already knew each other very well. To help me identify her when we met, at the Buckinghamshire Record Office in Aylesbury, Mary sent me a photograph. I showed it to my father and asked, 'Who do you think that is?' 'It's you,' he said, 'but I've never seen you in that yellow skirt.' So someone else could see what I had seen in the photograph, a marked similarity to myself in build and

Payments to William and John Batchelor.

features. Later, when I met Mary's aunt, her first words were, nodding towards me, 'Doesn't she favour your mother, Mary?' We have been asked on several occasions if we are sisters, and I still find it eerie looking at Mary's profile as she drives me to Hertford or Aylesbury on an ancestor hunt, for it is like seeing myself.

So when we met it was not as two strangers. We felt instantly at ease with one another and chattered happily together. When I went home with Mary I was introduced to her husband, Ernie, a long-suffering gentleman who thinks that we are both quite mad, spending so much time on people of the past. I think that he agrees with my mother that there is something morbid about dwelling on people who are long dead, but, as I said earlier, these people seem very much alive as we discover details of their joys and sorrows. Ernie's answer to our late-night sessions, as Mary and I chew over the seemingly insoluble problem of which William Batchelor married which Hannah, is simply to fall

Researching with Mary Geary.

asleep in his armchair until he hears the magic word, 'supper', crop up in our conversation. If only we could get him interested in *his* family. Then perhaps he would understand our obsession with the ancestors. After all, the Hertfordshire registers are full of Gearys living alongside our Batchelors.

Mary and Ernie have opened their home to me countless times on my regular visits south, and Mary's late mother's room has become, 'my room'. I regret never meeting Mary's mother, who was a Batchelor before her marriage, but I feel that she would be pleased that I used her room as my *pied-à-terre* when I research at Hertford or Aylesbury. Mary and I are very definitely kindred spirits, so it is hardly surprising that we have the same taste in so many areas. The first evening I arrived at her house she opened her cupboard to hang up my coat and I remarked, 'Oh, I have the same vacuum cleaner as you — even the same colour.' I went up to my room and found that it had the same lampshade as I have at home. In the bathroom were exactly the same toiletries. On the landing was an owl made from seashells, just like the one in *my* bathroom. In the spare room was the same seascape as I have at home. Mary's is a sunset picture and mine is moonlit, but it is the same beach, with identical rock formations, painted by the same artist.

Mary even has the identical cassette-player to the one I bought years ago for my mother. When we met at Penshurst Place, Kent, later in my adventure, we both turned up in clothes of the same colour — a combination of soft blues, greens and lilac. Neither of us had mentioned to the other what we were going to wear. No wonder we were twice asked that day, 'Are you two sisters?' Each of these incidents in itself may seem trivial but now, when I see yet again that we have the same taste in music or clothes or food, it no longer surprises me. We both feel so sure that we are distantly related and that our two family trees intertwine at some point in the past. After all, when my Batchelors were in the Chesham/Berkhamsted area, so were Mary's. If only we could solve the problem of the blessed Williams and Hannahs we would know for certain where the link comes. We have beavered away together in both the Herts. and Bucks. Record Offices but are no nearer to the answer.

We have studied, in detail, numerous Batchelor wills, for these can be very helpful. For a long time, at the start of my research, I had ignored wills altogether, thinking that my farming Batchelors would not be wealthy enough to make wills. How wrong I was. Even the poorest of them seems to have been concerned that their property fell into the right hands. Aylesbury has a wonderful collection of Batchelor wills for my area. My ancestors between 1527 and 1637 were indefatigable producers of wills. To me, wills are the most wonderful documents, for no dead person ever made a will. At the time of its production the man or woman concerned was still alive. We hear the voices of these living men and women across the centuries as they introduce themselves to us in the first line of their will:

'I, Hugh Bacheler of Rickmansworth—'
'I, Jone Bachiler of Saynte Leonards— Aston Clynton—'
'I, Robert Batchelor of Norcott Hill, husbandman—'
'I, John Batchelor of Rickmansworth, school-master—'

After a whole day studying their wills, I leave the Search Room with their voices still ringing in my ears. I have this mental picture of them all being put back into their dusty boxes from which the voices, now muffled, still call out:

'I, Thomas Bachelor of Porters—'
'I, Peter Bachelor of Hawridge—'
'I, Andrew Bachelor of St. Leonards—'
'I, Elizabeth Batchelor of Berkhamsted—'
'I, Edward Bachelor of St. Albans, innkeeper—'

My earliest female ancestor, Jone of St. Leonards, left an interesting will in 1555. In it she left the usual bequests to the church and to the poor of the parish, but also ten shillings 'to the mendyng of the highwaye between Aston and Aylesbury'. Her bequests to her family are very personal and, to me, quite touching.

'— to Joan — my dowter, my gowne, 3 sheets, 7 dishes, 7 platters, 2 candlesticks — one lesse, the other bigg.
— to Annes — my dowter, my kyrtell, a payer of sheets, on(e) panne, on(e) platt & xii dishes.
— to William Bachiler my sonne, my great spitte & to his wiff a payer of sheets.
— to John Bachiler my sonne, my great brase potte & to his wiff my great tubbe.'

I can just imagine the old farmer's wife looking around her home and thinking out her bequests so that there would be no arguments after her death about who should have the pots and pans. Her descendant, Peter Batchelor of Harridge, in his will made in 1660, left to his wife, Mary (née Twitchell), 'all my linen, brasse and pewter, and the Chest which was hers when she was a maid'. I suppose this was her bottom drawer, a chest of clothes and household linen which she brought with her when she married him. I find his mention of it very touching.

Wills can be extremely useful for confirming relationships. The will of John Bachiler of Berkhamsted, made in 1639, shows him leaving all his money to the children of his brother, Peter Batchelor of Hawridge. It also mentions his sister, Elizabeth, to whom he leaves 'all those goodes wch of right belonge unto mee nowe in the possession of Theophilus Royce her husband'.

Fascinating family feuds and arguments, too, are revealed in wills. In 1756 John Batchelor of Chesham Bois made an interesting will. In it he left, to his 'loving daughter, Mary Batchelor, the Sum of Twenty Pounds of Lawful Money of Great Britain — And also the Bed, Bedstead and all belonging thereto in the Bed Room and One Chest of Draws two pewter Dishes and three pewter Plates on this proviso — that if my said Daughter, Mary Batchelor, should ever be marryed to Charles Whitney then my mind and will is that my

Executor shall only give her One Shilling and nothing more and at the Expiration of the Six Months after my decease if she is not married at that time to give such security to my Executor as he thinks proper that she will never be Marryed to this said Charles Whitney before he pay the above mentioned Legacys'. She really would be cut off with a shilling if she married her Charles. I wonder what Father had against him? I wonder whether she defied her father and gave up her inheritance for love? One day, when I have time, I shall have a look for their wedding. I hate leaving a story incomplete.

It was the will of John Bachilor of Hawridge and Chesham, made in 1637, which showed the movement of my family across the Bucks./Herts. border. Edward Bacchelour, schoolmaster of Rickmansworth, was descended from Edward the innkeeper of St. Albans. Hertford Record Office had the will of Edward the innkeeper, signed with his mark, a large distinctive 'E'. At Aylesbury I saw the will of John Bachiler of Hawridge, Bucks. He bequeathed money to Peter Bachiler's children, all of whom were mentioned in the will of John of Berkhamsted. He also left money to his grandson, Jeames [sic], son of Theophilus Royce. John of Hawridge mentioned, almost as an afterthought, his other sons, John, Richard and Edward, whom he made executors of his last will and testament.

I was about to hand back the will when I noticed some more writing on the back. I thought at first that this was the usual confirmation of the proving of the will in the ecclesiastical court. Then the words, 'late of Hawridge, deceased', caught my eye and I realised that here was something in English, not the formal legal Latin I had expected. I struggled to decipher the spidery writing with its numerous alterations, convinced that it would reveal something important. After a great deal of effort I finally read the whole paragraph:

'We, John Batchelor, Richard Batchelor and Edward Batchelor, executors of the last will and testament of John Batchelor, late of Hawridge,

Will of Andrew of St. Leonards, 1527.
'In the name of God, amen. I, Andrew Bacheler of the parish of Aston
Clynton in the county of Bucks, yoeman, make this my testament and last
will on Saint Mark's Day the 19th year of the reign of King Henry VIII.'

deceased, are contented to pay for the proveinge of the will and makeinge pfect of the inventories the summe of 6s.10d. And whereas I, Richard Batchelor, used some ill language about the paeing thereof, doe acknowledge my selfe to be sorye for the same and would not utter the same speeces if they were to be spoken again.'

There I hear the voice of a true Batchelor across the centuries, objecting in no uncertain terms to being overcharged. We never lie down under an injustice, but in this case poor Richard had to eat humble pie. What made this such an exciting discovery were the signatures of the three brothers. Richard's mark was a rather wobbly 'R', John's badly written 'J' was lying face down and wrongly attributed to Edward, but Edward's mark was the one which interested me. His bold, clear 'E', very neatly drawn, was exactly like that on the will of my ancestor, Edward the innkeeper of St. Albans. Thus, in my search for my family, I was led across the county border from Hertfordshire and into Buckinghamshire.

Deposited along with wills there are often inventories. I think these are my favourite documents. They satisfy the 'nosey parker' in me, who wants to know what my ancestors had in their rooms and cupboards. When someone died, trusted friends of the family or neighbours were given the task of making a list of every item in the house. Every plate and spoon had to be listed, every sheet and napkin, every stick of furniture and all the pots and pans. The inventory, carefully listed room by room, takes you on a tour of the house.

When William Bachelor of North Church died in 1610, the inventory of his goods was drawn up by 'Willm Edlyn, Willm Willet, Raffe Axtill, John Mooris, John England and others'. Among other things they listed his stock:

'13 hennes, one cock and fyve chickens, one hog, two plow horses, xv sheep, ewes and pygges'.

In the yard were:

'two rotten dong cartes, 2 ould + broken paire of wheeles'.

and other bits and pieces of farm equipment. In the barn they noted hay, oats and wheat. Inside the house were axes, pitchforks, mattocks and bills, along with 'an ould rusty sword' valued at iis.vid. (2/6d.). In the other loft was 'a p(ar)cell of wooll allmost spoilld with moths', valued at xiiis.iiiid. (13/4d.). In the hall, the main living area, William had:

'3 pothangers, a payer of cobyrons, a payer of andyrons, a dripping pan, a fryeing pan … a payer of tonges, a payer of bellowes wth som more sory things about the chimney'.

The only other items in the room worth mentioning seemed to be 'an ould chayre and three stooles'. Among other things in the bedchamber were a hammer, three

19

chisels and 'the tynes of an ould pytchfork'. His pewter was valued at xxs. (20/-) and included:

'12 platters, 2 frute dyshes + 21 pewter spoones'.

He also had 'a small oulde saw dekayed wth rust'. There were 'two flitches of Bacon in the chimney', obviously in the process of being smoked, and two more 'in the salt trowgh'.

In the lower chamber William had 'a plain bedsted of bordes wth sory bedding on yt', and in the same room, 'a gryndston, 2 ould payles and a wheel'. There were two more old pitchfork tynes here. Probably he was going to give them all new handles one day. I, too, find it difficult to throw broken things away. It must be a family failing. In spite of the sorry state of William's belongings, his wearing apparel was valued at xls. (40/-) which was a considerable amount of money in 1610. The total value of his property was given as £46.17s.11d. (or £46.90p. in today's currency). The

complete inventory, neatly written, covers three pages. The picture we get from it is of a large, rather run-down, working farm.

In contrast the complete inventory of one John Bachelor of Tring, Herts., in 1618 lists:

'In primis his apparell	40s.
Item one coverlide	10s.
Item one brass pan	6s.8d.
Item a pot + pothangers	4s.
Item a ploughshare + old iron	5s.
Item one chest	6s.
Item a salt trough	4s. '

This inventory is smudged and torn and yet it has survived. Its very brevity reminds us of the contrast between our comfortable home life and the spartan living conditions of some of our ancestors.

Others led more affluent lives. In 1640 Edward Bachelor, the innkeeper of St. Albans, was a master of

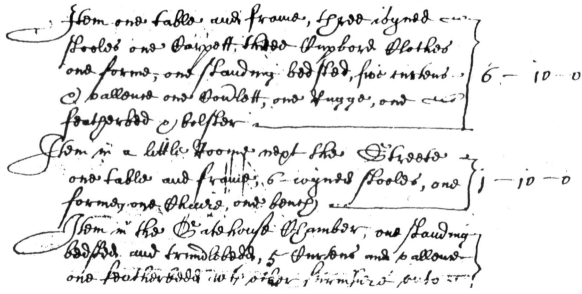

Extract from Inventory of Edward Bachelour, innkeeper of St. Albans
(1640).

a fine, well-furnished house, with numerous rooms for his guests. Many were equipped with a trundle bed, stored under the standing bedstead with its curtains and vallance. If a guest should be sharing his room with his servant, or a child, then the spare bed on wheels was 'trundled out' for their use. In a number of rooms I came across references to 'painted cloths'. At first I thought I must have misread the document. Could it be 'patched clothes'? Then I discovered that painted cloths were used by people who could not afford real tapestry hangings for their walls. At a distance a painted cloth could give the illusion of a tapestry picture. Edward's inn had carpets and cushions, feather-beds and leather stools. A grand place to stay when visiting the shrine of the martyred saint, Alban, and a far cry from William's house with its plain 'bedsted of bordes wth sory bedding on yt'.

Of course, I should mention here that early wills and inventories are not easy to read. The first time I saw an early 17th-century inventory I could hardly believe that it was written in English. The writer had used a different alphabet from the one we use today. I felt so frustrated, for here was a message from the past and I had no idea what it was trying to say to me. Fortunately the young man at the Hertford Record Office was kind enough to go through it with me and introduce me to the mysteries of the writing called Secretary Hand. Later, at the Society of Genealogists in London, I bought myself a wonderful little book called, *An ABC of Secretary Hand,* which has proved invaluable to me. Using it, I taught myself to decipher the early Batchelor wills and parish registers. Painstakingly, like a child learning to read, I spelled out the words, letter by letter, out loud, and a whole new world of exciting discoveries opened up to me. Now Peter of Hawridge and Andrew of St. Leonards could get their messages to me across the centuries. To be able to read for myself the thoughts and wishes of my people helps to bring them to life in my mind's eye, and puts flesh on the bones. They are not merely names on a family tree but real people whose existence is confirmed when their parish registers list their baptisms, marriages and burials.

Of course, some early documents are faded with age or damaged by water stains, or else very badly written and covered with ink blots and crossings-out. Eve McLaughlin, of the Buckinghamshire Family History Society and writer of the excellent *McLaughlin Guides,* puts it so well when she says, 'Your ancestors liked living in parishes where the clerk wrote up the registers with a pitchfork dipped in soot!' How true! When I find myself confronted with such a register, the teacher in me wants to send it back to the clerk with the comment, written in red ink, 'This is not good enough. Write it out again — *neatly.*'

Learning Secretary Hand was like teaching myself a new language. It is immensely satisfying now to take an old document and be able to read it quite fluently. I find it thrilling to be able to tackle documents written when Henry VIII was king or when the first Elizabeth was on the throne. This skill was to prove invaluable to me, much later in my research, when I made the amazing discovery that my family did produce someone famous, and I found myself confronted with official court documents from the time of Queen Elizabeth. This was to prove the most colourful and exciting part of my family research. However, that was all to come later. My one burning ambition at this point in my adventure was 'to do an Alex Haley' — to return to my roots.

Chapter Three

Returning to my Roots

'In age I find myself with an interest in my forebears which I never felt when I was young.'
Graham Greene.

It was an eerie sensation, standing on the platform of Berkhamsted railway station and seeing the name, so familiar to me from parish registers, now staring me in the face in letters a foot high. So there really was such a place. The girls at Woodcock Travel had never heard of it but here I was at last. It was from here that my George and Eliza set forth on *their* adventure, travelling north to a new life in York. Now I was reversing the process, travelling south into the unknown.

I had written to the Berkhamsted local library for advice on accommodation, and they had sent me a list of inns and guesthouses, from which I selected the Goat Inn. It was an old drovers' inn situated on the A41, the ancient Roman Akeman Street which runs straight through Berkhamsted and on to London. The librarian also sent me a street map so that I could find my way about. At this point I feel I should pay tribute to our library services. Whenever I visit a strange town in pursuit of my ancestors, my first move is usually a letter to the local library for a map and advice on accommodation. Their help has been invaluable to me, for they are the fount of all local knowledge and will often volunteer additional information over and above what I have requested.

I felt a shiver of excitement as I stood outside the Goat Inn, for there in the distance I could see the church of St. Peter, where my great-grandfather, George, was baptised and my 2xgreat-grandparents, his father and mother, Joseph and Hannah, were married. Quickly I dumped my luggage in the Goat's cottage across the road, where I was to spend the next few nights, and went to the bar for a light lunch. The whole room was festooned with a wonderful collection of Toby jugs and in the garden at the back was an aviary of brightly coloured tropical birds whose twittering and whistling gave the old inn a most un-English atmosphere.

I made sure that the young lady behind the bar knew why I was there and sat down with my lunch to await developments. I saw her lean towards a small group of locals at the bar and heard the name, 'Batchelor'. There was some muttering and a great deal of head-shaking. No one appeared to know any present day Berkhamsted Batchelors. I couldn't help remembering how Graham Greene described the Berkhamsted men he saw in his childhood, when his father was the Headmaster of Berkhamsted School. He said that they were small-featured and sly-faced. Those men at the bar did have the same characteristics — the dark, pinched face I had seen in photographs of my grandfather, whose father was a Berkhamsted man born and bred. Strange, too, that in the Army my father was known as 'Foxy Batchelor' because he could be quite cunning at times.

Having drawn a blank at the inn, I made my way to the church where so many of my family had been before me. I sat in the silent church and remembered James steering the heavily pregnant Frances Bird up the aisle in 1811, trying to get her to the altar before the stork delivered my 2xgreat-grandfather, little Joseph. It is at moments like this that time seems to telescope down and I have the distinct feeling that they have only just left — that I have just missed them by a few minutes.

On a later visit to the church, when I had brought my parents with me so that my father could experience a return to *his* roots, I made an interesting discovery. Behind the present altar was the original sanctuary, a place of broken chairs and old hymn-books. Against the wall was a very old and very beautiful painting of the crucifixion. Could this be the original altar before which James made an honest woman of his Frances? Later the poor soul was brought here for her burial at the tragically early age of 22. I found myself imagining

James, his grief tinged with panic at the prospect of caring for three small children on his own.

This, for me, is real family research. It means trying to get behind the dates and events to the thoughts and feelings of the people involved. It struck me very forcibly when I first started studying parish records and came upon pitiful entries such as:

'Buried — a poore travailing woman unknowne, dieing at Ly Green.'

or

'Buried — Minnie Harrap aged 10 years
George U. Harrap aged 4 months
John Harrap aged 4 months'

Who was she — that lonely, nameless woman? What was her story? And what childhood illness carried off little Minnie and her two baby brothers? How we still feel for these people, even when separated from them by many centuries. We grieve for the mother who carried her child the full nine months, only to lose him at birth. We feel for the widow who loses a well-loved

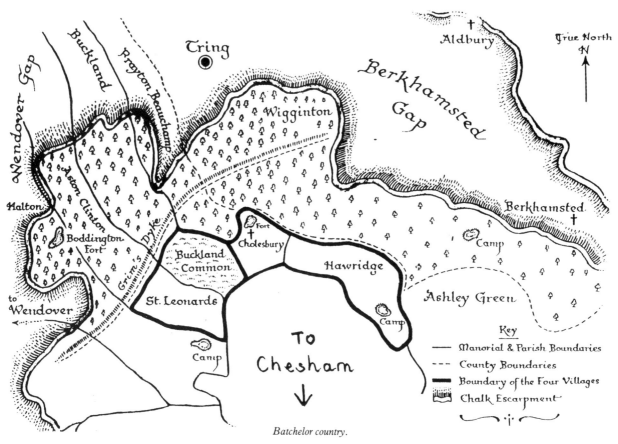

Batchelor country.

23

and hard-working son:

'BERKHAMSTED DEANERY MAGAZINE
(1903-4)

In Memoriam

The very greatest sympathy is felt for Mrs. Batchelor and her family in their very great sorrow. Neighbours and friends in various ways are doing their best to help the crushed mother to bear her grief. It is some comfort to the mother to hear of the great respect felt for her son by his master Mr. Tayler of Nettleden and his family. The grief felt at Nettleden Farm is like grief felt for the loss of a son. It is indeed a sadness for a young man in the prime of life suddenly to be cut off. We all feel and pray for them.'

So as we busy ourselves with our research, we discover that we are not learning about historical characters but people like ourselves, experiencing the same pleasures and pain, joy and grief, as we do.

Stepping out of St. Peter's into the afternoon sunshine, I noticed a G.N.R. John Batchelor on the war memorial. Who was he, I wondered. To my great disappointment the old churchyard was completely grassed over and the modern cemetery nearby, though containing a number of Batchelors, had none related to me as far as I could see. I did notice a moving inscription for a Fanny Batchelor who died in 1945 aged 90:

'There is a link death cannot sever,
Love and remembrance last forever.
Sleep on, dear Mother, thy labours o'er,
Thy willing hands will toil no more.
A loving mother true and kind,
No friend on earth like thee we'll find.'

There, too, was her seven-year-old grandson, another John Batchelor, who was 'called away' in 1925:

'God has saved from weary strife,
In its dawn this fresh young life.'

I wondered what weary strife he might have seen had he lived. Certainly he would have experienced some amazing changes in the years since 1925. Television links with the other side of the world and men walking on the moon, heart transplants and microwave cooking. I often think that if my ancestors could return for one day they would think that our daily lives were run by magic. Only two generations ago my Grandma Batchelor refused to have electricity in her home because she was afraid that it would leak out of the sockets. My father well remembers going to bed by candlelight in the 1920s and this in the heart of a modern city.

It was getting late now and would soon be dark, so I took just a short walk along the High Street which links Berkhamsted with the neighbouring village of North Church. As the High Street nears North Church it changes its name to Gossoms End. This was the road on which Great-great-grandfather Joseph lived with his wife, Hannah, and their children. They appear on the 1841 census as an 'ag.lab.' (agricultural labourer) and a straw plaiter. In 1851 and all the later census records he gives his occupation as 'gardener'. My great-grandfather, George, first appears in the Gossoms End records in 1851 as a seven-year-old scholar, but by 1861 he is working as a carter.

Another interesting bit of information came to light as I studied the Gossoms End census. The family are shown as living next door but one to the Stag beerhouse in 1851, but had moved up to a smaller house next door to the Stag by 1861. In the High Street I had bought a book of Old Berkhamsted from a local historian, Percy Birchnell. In it I found a photograph taken outside the Stag. It is, sadly, undated but shows a large group of 24 people including a number of children. They smile towards the camera in the self-conscious way we no longer see in modern photography. All the males, even the smallest boy aged about six, wear flat cloth caps. The girls wear large sunbonnets and button boots. The houses adjoining the Stag can be seen clearly. I found myself wondering whether any of these lads or lasses were Batchelors. Perhaps, without knowing it, I have here a photograph of young George, my great-grandfather. Could one of the bonny lasses be Eliza, soon to be his bride? How frustrating not to know.

A chance find at the Hertford Record Office gave me a detailed description of the home of my Batchelors. It was a bill of sale dated 1869. It tells how the recently widowed Mrs. Holliman occupied the beer house, and describes the adjoining cottage where Joseph and Hannah had lived as, 'a brick built and slated cottage containing a large dwelling house, kitchen and two good bedrooms over, large yard with side entrance — a large garden extending to the river and overlooking the park of the late Col. Finch, having a frontage of 230 feet 6 inches to Water Lane. There is a pump with well of excellent water on the premises. This property — is copyhold of the Duchy of Cornwall, the Halimote of North Church, Parcel of the Honour of Berkhamstead.' How lucky to have found such a detailed description of their two-up, two-down home.

I set off the next morning to walk from the Goat at Berkhamsted, along Gossoms End to North Church, to see whether I could locate the Stag. It was a bright and sunny morning, but with a gusty wind which should have warned me of the rain to come. I passed the site of the Old Royal Oak public house which had been kept by another Joseph and Hannah Batchelor. Their burial records had caused me great confusion until I realised that there *were* two Josephs and Hannahs. A few years later I was to have the same problem with no fewer than five William Batchelors who all chose to marry ladies by the name of Hannah within a comparatively short space of time. Hannahs Dell, Halliday, Field, Ambrose and Culverhouse were all wooed and wed by William Batchelors.

There was no sign of the Stag beerhouse on Gossoms End. My street plan of Berkhamsted showed Stag Lane, which was probably the more recent name of Water Lane mentioned on the Stag bill of sale. However, Stag Lane was no longer there. Only a small road leading to a factory showed where it might have been. To my great delight, there was a small group of terrace houses nearby, one of which had not been completely modernised. Its exterior showed exactly the same arrangement of doors and windows as those I had seen in the photograph in Percy Birchnell's book. I felt that I had come very close to the place where my great-grandfather had been born. It was very satisfying.

A few more minutes' walk brought me to North Church. I was quite prepared to find that it was now an area of modern housing but to my great excitement I saw that the church stood in an old churchyard, on one side of which were some beautiful timbered houses. This was the church where my George and his Eliza were married before their move to York. Here old Theophilus was christened. How strange to think of him as a tiny baby! Here my naughty James buried his 13-year-old daughter who bore my name, Ann Batchelor. His Frances had died 11 years earlier when Ann was a baby. Who, I wondered, had brought up her children? Surely not James, who would have had to go to work to provide for his family. Did some close female relative care for the motherless Joseph, Elizabeth and Ann? Already I was discovering that the more information the family historian gathers, the more avid becomes the thirst for detail.

I walked down the long path to the church door, very conscious that I was retracing my ancestors' steps as they went with joy to their weddings, with pride to their christenings and in grief to their funerals. I put my hand to the church door and — calamity! It was locked. Had I come so far only to be turned back at the door? Of course, had I planned my visit properly I would have written to the churchwardens to ask for access to the church. It was a hard lesson to learn. I would know better next time.

Gloomily I made my way across the road, through the seemingly endless stream of heavy traffic going Londonwards in clouds of dust and fumes. In the village post office I bought a few postcards of the old timbered houses. Casually I remarked on the weather. 'Looks like rain, doesn't it? At least it's warmer here than it was when I left Leeds.' Why do the English always discuss the weather, I wonder? I then made an interesting discovery. This English idiosyncrasy is an extremely useful way of leading a conversation round to what you really want to say. The lady behind the counter asked what brought me all the way from Leeds. I told her that my great-grandparents had been married at North Church. 'I was hoping to go inside the church,' I said, 'but the door is locked.' 'That's no problem,' she told me. 'Jack Reynolds has the key. He lives in the house next to the church.' With mounting excitement I took my life in my hands and re-crossed the A41.

Mr. Reynolds was out, his wife told me, but he would be back shortly. Perhaps I would like to look round the churchyard? I must admit here that I love old churchyards. They, more than any other historical source, give the character of a town or village. Here you find the families who have toiled in the fields for many generations, now resting with the prayer, 'O Lord, abide with me'. Here you can see the ostentatious tombs of the well-to-do, even in death trying to outdo their neighbours. Here are the simple graves of small children with their stone angels and plaintive inscriptions: 'We have not forgotten you'. 'Till we meet again'.

There is one remarkable inhabitant of the churchyard at North Church. A very simple stone marks the grave of Peter the Wild Boy. Peter had been found living wild in a field near Hamelin, Germany, and was brought to England in 1725. His lack of speech and wild appearance made him a great novelty and he was brought to the court of George I. From there he was sent to live with a Mr. and Mrs. Fenn at their farm at Broadway, on the outskirts of Berkhamsted. He found life on the farm restrictive and was inclined to wander off, so he was made to wear a collar bearing his name and address. People would come great distances to see him, plying him with drink and laughing at his attempts at singing. A waxworks effigy was made of him and was exhibited in London. He died in his seventies and lies just outside the church door of St. Mary's.

As I waited for Mr. Reynolds to materialise I studied the oldest stones in the churchyard. Here I found members of the Pitkin family, whose names crop up regularly as witnesses to some of my 17th-century Batchelor wills. It felt like meeting old friends. Then a new friend arrived in the person of Jack Reynolds, a beaming gentleman who was delighted to open the church door for me. He watched in quiet amusement as I took a deep breath and crossed the threshold into my family's past.

The church was cool and bright with sunshine which now shone through the windows. I stood before the altar and thought of George and Eliza starting their married life together here, never dreaming that in ten years time they would be far away in York. What a contrast that would be, from the open fields of North Church and Berkhamsted to the heat of the glassworks and the squalor of Paver Lane. On the wall of the church was an oil painting of North Church as it was before the advent of the motorcar and continental juggernaut. The church, neat and white, is surrounded by a cluster of houses and cottages. In the fields nearby, 'ag.labs.' harvest the corn by hand. The atmosphere is quiet and calm. St. Mary's was the parent church of St. Peter's, Berkhamsted, originally. Later Berkhamsted expanded with factories and the railway. St. Peter's became the more prosperous church while St. Mary's retained the atmosphere of a village church.

Jack Reynolds showed me the parish chest where, in the past, registers were kept. Now, of course, they are deposited at the County Record Office in Hertford. Then we adjourned to the pub across the road, where he introduced me to a number of interested inhabitants of the village, none of whom were able to tell me anything about my Batchelors. Jack was the first of many total strangers who, over the years, were to welcome me to their patch and whose enthusiasm and helpfulness have added greatly to the enjoyment of my adventure.

After a fine bar lunch he left me to potter round the churchyard on my own. To my great delight I made a discovery there. I found a large brown stone whose weathered and lichen covered inscription was almost illegible, but by using my fingertips I was able to make out the name 'BATCHELOR'. Then, by moving to the side so that the shadows were cast deeper, I read 'SARAH' and a date which looked like 1866. I had no idea who she was at the time, but later Jack cleaned up the stone sufficiently to be able to read the full inscription and date: 'December 30 1866, aged 60 years'. I believe that she is Sarah Staples, who married Charles Batchelor, but where she fits on my tree is anyone's guess. She is filed away as one of my odd-bods and, like one of those frustrating pieces of jigsaw which don't seem to fit anywhere, she awaits the moment when she can be fitted into the space where she belongs.

At this point the rain, which had been waiting in the wings, now descended as though the heavens had opened. The churchyard soon became what Tudor folk called 'oozie, slubbie and glibsey grounde'. As I squelched my way across the sodden grass I regretted my earlier decision to wear comfortable sandals for my walk from Berkhamsted. With rain running down my face and turning my notebook to papier maché, I took shelter in the church, where I found myself in the company of the flower ladies who were preparing the church for Sunday. Flower ladies and volunteer church cleaners are invaluable to the family historian, for they are keepers of village gossip.

'Batchelors?' they said, and began to reel off a list of Batchelors they had known. As I scribbled frantically in my notebook, I found it difficult to keep pace with them. If only I had learnt to write shorthand. 'Annie and May Batchelor,' they said, 'and old Edward who lived in Sunnside. Then do you remember Walter and Rose? Their son was John. And Lionel and Horace — I went to school with them,' and they laughed at the memories those names brought back. All those names are still in my notebook, awaiting the moment when they, too, will slot into their place in my genealogical jigsaw.

A church like St. Mary's is a time-capsule. There the past rubs shoulders with the present. On one of the stone columns I found graffiti almost three centuries old. How strange it is that the graffiti which sickens us in our own time delights us if it originates in the distant past. There, scratched on the stone, I saw the name of JOHN ROLFE and the date 1713. My old Theophilus of York had been born at North Church to James Batchelor, and his wife, Elizabeth (née Rolfe). She would have been born around 1800, so that John Rolfe could perhaps be her great-grandfather. Certainly, living in such a small community, he would be likely to be of the same family. It is fun to speculate but not, of course, serious geneaology. Perhaps one day I shall have time to research the Rolfes properly — or perhaps not. Sadly, one lifetime is hardly long enough to discover the answers to all my genealogical questions.

Having seen both Berkhamsted and North Church, my family pilgrimage now led me further south. Again I had the thrill of seeing a familiar name appear across my railway carriage window. This time the magical name was Rickmansworth. I had booked myself into a small hotel for a couple of nights, knowing very little about my Rickmansworth Batchelors except for their presence here in the early 18th century. I had also found the will of a John Batchelor, schoolmaster of Rickmansworth, at Hertford, but doubted whether he was one of mine. In the year 1749 he left his cottages at Dell Hall to his wife, Martha. My Batchelors had, so far, proved to be merely farm labourers and nothing so grand as a village schoolmaster.

I strolled around the churchyard of St. Mary's where my Rickmansworth Batchelors were buried. An inscription to John and Margaret Morley caught my eye. Sternly they warned me:

'Stay, mortal, stay as you go alone.
One moment stay to read this stone.
Death did to us short warning give.
Therefore be careful how you live.'

Having made a note of their advice from beyond the

grave, I entered the church to find an army of cleaners scrubbing and polishing. I told them of my quest and received the now familiar enthusiastic response. They knew of no present-day Batchelors, but a helpful old gentleman directed me up to Chorleywood Road where he thought I might find my Dell Hall cottages.

I had a brisk walk on that golden autumn afternoon, past the modern cemetery, until I reached a small group of cottages now called Bankside Down. I had no way of knowing whether these were indeed John Batchelor's cottages. The only person at home that afternoon was not able to tell me anything about the age of the buildings. I wandered aimlessly around the area for some time, peering in at a gate marked, 'Dell House', but was frightened off by all the Neighbourhood Watch notices. After all, I *was* behaving in a very suspicious manner. Who would believe me if I gave the lame excuse that I was looking for cottages mentioned in a will almost 250 years ago? I decided to call it a day, before someone notified the local constabulary.

The next morning I made the inspired decision to visit the Rickmansworth Public Library. There I asked the librarian for details of any local history group who might be able to help me. 'That lady over there would know,' she said. 'She is an official of the Rickmansworth Local History Society. Let me introduce you.' She led me across the room and introduced me to Diane Rattle, whose immediate response was, 'Oh, you *must* get in touch with Wilf.' She gave me the address of a man who was to become a good friend and a great help to me over the next few years. As Wilf was away from home that week, I had to be content with writing him a letter about my Batchelors, including the names of my 9xgreat-grand-parents, Edward and Rachel. Within a few days I received his reply. I still remember standing in the hall of my flat on my return from work one evening, avidly reading it before I had even removed my coat. Here, at last, was someone who actually knew something about my Rickmansworth Batchelors.

To me, at this stage of my research, they were merely names culled from the parish registers. Wilf's letter changed all that. He told me that my Edward and Rachel were the first master and mistress of the Rickmansworth Charity School when it opened in 1711. So my 9xgreat-grandparents had been teachers like myself. Perhaps, inherited from them, I had chalk in my blood? Certainly no other Batchelors had been teachers, apart from their son, John, of the Dell Hall cottages. I was descended from them through their second son, another Edward.

Back in the Hertford Record Office I asked whether they had any records of the Rickmansworth Charity School. All they had was the accounts book. This contained an explanation of the reason for setting up the school:

'Whereas the prophaness and debauchery are great owing to a gross ignorance of the Christian religion among the poorer sort, and whereas nothing is more likely to promote the practise of Christianity and vertue than an early and pious education of youth, and whereas many poore people are desirous of haveing their children taught but are not able to afford a Christian and useful education — We whose names are underwritten do hereby agree to pay yearly at 4 ¼ly payments the several sums of money over against our names respectively subscribed for the setting up of a Charity School in the Parish of Rickmansworth — for teaching poor children to read and instructing them in the knowledge and practise of the Christian religion as professed and taught in the Church of England, and for learning such other things as are suitable to their condition and capacity.'

This was followed by a list of subscribers and the amount of money each one promised. The book also recorded payments to my teacher ancestors. Edward received his last payment in April 1716 but his death was recorded in January 1716. At first I could not understand why, when he died in January, payments continued until April. Then I learnt that, until 1753, the New Year began on 25 March. So Edward's last payment in April 1716 came nine months before his death in January 1716. The year 1717 did not begin until March. To simplify matters, events which occur between 1 January and 25 March before 1753 are usually double dated. That is, Edward died in January 1716/17. Very confusing at first, but quite a useful thing to remember, for this difference in dating can make interesting revelations about our families.

For instance, Edward and Rachel, the school-teachers, were married in Fulmer, Bucks., on 28 January 1691. Their first son, John, was baptised in Rickmansworth, Herts., on 13 April 1692. Quite a respectable gap between marriage and the first child — if the year in January. But as it started in *March*, April 1692 was only the fourth month after January, 1691. Perhaps this explains them marrying out of their own area. Fulmer's registers for that time show a large number of 'stray' marriages, with brides and grooms from places as far apart as Hammersmith and Farnham Royal, Langley and Brackenfield, and from parishes which had perfectly good parish churches of their own, such as Windsor, Iver and Chalfont St. Peter. It has been suggested to me that Fulmer was a Chapel of Convenience, where marriages could be performed at short notice with no questions asked. A good idea if Rachel was indeed six months pregnant when she

married. That would explain them settling in Rickmansworth, where there would be few people who knew them, and where the new Parish Clerk could arrive with his heavily pregnant wife without anyone knowing how recent had been their wedding.

The Charity School accounts book, which I saw at Hertford, was rather battered. The binding felt loose and I turned to the back to see how secure it was. Imagine my delight on discovering, inside the back cover, my Rachel signing receipts for her wages:

'January 2nd 1717 Recd then of Willm Wankford Treasurer of the Charity Schoole the sume of two pounds for one quarter teaching the girles due at Xmas last — Rachel Batchelor'

The entries, three in all, are probably in Rachel's own hand, for they are written in the old style Secretary Hand. The treasurer, too, is referred to in a familiar way, as Will Wankford. The teacher of the boys that year, Ed Dyson, was obviously a younger man who wrote in a more modern style and was more respectful to 'Mr. Wankford'.

I often feel as though, in some strange way, my ancestors stand in the shadows of Time, watching my pitiful attempts to discover their story. Just occasionally I feel as though my outstretched fingers almost reach them. This moment, as I held the book Rachel had held and saw her handwriting, was one such moment, — what I call 'a finger-tip experience'. In June 1722, in an absentminded moment, she signed herself, 'Rachelor Batchelor'. Poor Rachel can be forgiven, for, after a hectic day 'teaching the girles', I, too, have been known to write rubbish. I remember writing the name, 'Richard Batchelor', and finding that the 'ch' had led me into writing, 'Richelor'. It was quite touching to come across this little sign of humanity in the rather formal accounts book. It would be fascinating to discover how Rachel came to be so well educated. Ann Bath, who replaced her in 1728, could not even write her own name and had to sign for her wages with a mark.

Signature of Rachel, the schoolmistress.

Some years later, in 1734, the subscribers do not appear to have kept their promise to support the school, and a note is made that John, the son of Edward and Rachel, could not be paid in full:

'October 1734
Received for the £2 that was behind — £1/14/0d — all that can be paid thro' the deficiency of the subscriptions — by me John Batchelor'.

Funds seem to have been forthcoming in 1737 when John received:

'the ¼age due last Midsummer for teaching the Charity boys and at the same time 16 shillings and sixpence for Paper, Pens, Ink used in teaching the said boys to write.
I say rec. by me — John Batchelor'.

Among the archives at Hertford I found two letters from the Vicar of Rickmansworth, John James. He was a great writer of begging letters on behalf of the school. One, to Mr. Henry Newman at the Revd. Mr. Shute's house in Bartlet Buildings, in Holborn, is dated 28 January 1711, and reads:

'Your Charity to our School In giving Books to the poor children for their Instruction in Religion Encourages Me to beg of you Some more, viz: the Church Catechism Explained by Mr. John Henry which I judge very fitt to lead them to the Understanding of Religion and Some of the Small tracts — A Pastoral Letter — to take care of their Souls.
Yr Obleiged, Obedt. Servt,
Jo: James'.

It would be a hard man indeed who could resist such a plea. One of the skills which the family historian must develop is the ability to write such letters, begging not for money but for assistance in the hunt for the ancestors. I could not have made the progress I have without the extreme kindness and helpfulness of those people to whom I have sent my written cries for help. Replies such as the one I had from Wilf Broughton are

Wilf Broughton of Rickmansworth.

the stuff of which exciting discoveries are made — a source of great delight adding a thrill to the ancestor-hunt.

Wilf is a mine of information about early Rickmansworth, in spite of being a Yorkshireman. I well remember the first time we met, after corresponding for almost a year. We arranged that he would meet me at Rickmansworth station. I wrote, jokingly, 'This is rather like one of those old spy movies. For identification we should meet under the clock and each wear a red carnation!' Just for fun, as my train drew into Rickmansworth, I took from my pocket a red silk carnation and pinned it to my coat. The train drew to a halt and I alighted, to find myself confronted by a smiling gentleman — red carnation blazing in his buttonhole. Our laughter broke the ice of what could have been a rather formal meeting, and I was whisked away to meet Ethel, who welcomed me into her home with the same warm and generous hospitality which I have received time and time again throughout my adventure.

I had a little smile to myself, some time later, when I read of a young lady who replied to an advertisement for a wife in a Bucks. newspaper in 1889. She wrote to the lonely gentleman, promising to meet him at Chesham station at 8.30pm on Thursday, adding that she would wear three white roses and suggesting that he wore a red geranium. Apparently between three and four hundred people were at the station to see them meet — only to discover that the whole thing was a hoax.

Thankfully my meeting with Wilf was no hoax. From him I learnt more about my Rickmansworth Batchelors and their Charity School. He, too, introduced me to my lovely Emily Batchelor of the wild hair and short petticoats — but more of her in a later chapter. Before I returned home I visited the churchyard of St. Mary's, where both Edward and Rachel are buried. 'Edward Batchelor — Buryed 29 Jan 1716', says the register. 'Rachel Batchelor, widow, in woollen only, September 3 1727'. This refers to Rachel's woollen shroud, used to comply with the current legislation, passed to help the English wool trade.

Coincidentally, a French stained-glass window from Rickmansworth, removed during the restoration of the church, found its way to York Minster. I wonder whether any of my York Batchelors ever saw it? Even if they did, they could not have known that their early ancestors had worshipped in its light.

My hunt for my ancestors now led me to Chesham in Buckinghamshire. I had discovered that my family had crossed the Bucks./Herts. border around 1638, when Edward, descended from John Bachelor of Chesham, married at St. Albans. Before that date my ancestral family had lived in the Chesham/Hawridge/Aston Clinton area. Once again I made my first contact via the post. I wrote to the churchwarden of St. Mary's, Chesham, for confirmation that one of my family, Peter Bachelor, had married Mary Twitchell at that church in 1619. I asked whether the registers were still at the church and enclosed a small donation for the church, something I always do out of courtesy. After all, it is hardly right to expect someone to do research for nothing and, in my experience, officers of the church such as vergers and churchwardens are often extremely busy people.

In reply I had a most helpful letter from a Mr. Piggin, who was to become another of those special friends without whom my research would have ground to a halt. I wrote again, asking whether I could see the actual registers if I came to Chesham in person, and also whether Mr. Piggin could recommend a small guest house where I could book bed and breakfast. Back came the now familiar warm invitation to accept hospitality, this time 'chez Piggin'. As my train rushed me through the Bucks. countryside, I felt like a time-traveller. After all, I was now returning to my 17th-century roots. 'Who knows where this journey will lead?' I asked myself. I gazed out of my carriage window and found myself wondering whether any of my family had worked in the fields around me.

On Chesham station, this time minus red carnation, I was collected by George Piggin, the man I now think of as 'The Cheerful Churchwarden of Chesham'. One of the great delights of my research has been meeting some of Life's great enthusiasts. From verger to local historian, churchwarden to early music specialist, my recent years have been brightened by the incandescence of their enthusiasm. George's speciality is old Chesham. He gives talks, conducts tours of the town and answers masses of letters such as mine, as well as helping to run a massive parish of around 22,000 souls.

Chesham is rapidly expanding but trying desperately to retain its original market-town character as it becomes, almost against its will, a prosperous dormitory development for London commuters. Its

My cheerful churchwarden of Chesham: George Piggin and his wife, Mary.

town motto is a Biblical one: 'By love serve one another'. In the past it had its share of colourful characters. There was the brave Thomas Harding, the last Lollard martyr, who was burned at the stake in what is now called Martyr's Dell at White Hill in 1532. Then there was the famous 17th-century hermit, Roger Crab, know as the Mad Hatter, who dressed in sackcloth, ate grass and turnip tops, lived on ¾d per week and gave his money to the poor. Chesham folk have always been rugged individualists, strong-willed and determined. Perhaps this is where my father and I get our fierce independence and determination to 'do it *my* way'. In the more recent past Chesham was a famous spa for those with 'skin diseases, general debility, groaning of the stomache and gravelly troubles'.

My friend, George Piggin, is a wonderful source of Chesham information and has some lovely anecdotes gathered during his years at St. Mary's. My favourite story concerns a Chinese lady who arrived at his door one day carrying a small cloth bag. She spoke no English, but her son explained that she was the widow of a Welshman who had gone to live in China many years ago. Though he had become, to all intents and purposes, Chinese, he had always said that when his time came he wanted to be buried in an English churchyard. He had since died and here (holding up the little bag) were his ashes. Would George be kind enough to arrange for their burial? Never at a loss when faced with the unexpected, George rose to the occasion and arranged a brief service in the church before the committal. 'It was,' he told me with a smile, 'the first, and probably the last, time that the ancient walls of St. Mary's had echoed to the words of the Lord's Prayer in Chinese!'

George took me up the hill to the church to see the old registers for myself. With loving care he removed them from the fireproof, damp-proof, rodent-proof safe which the regulations dictate must be provided if the registers are to be kept at the church. After all, it is a well-known fact that church mice will use anything handy for nesting material, and how are they to know that a 16th-century register is something special?

In fact, St. Mary's registers go back to 1538 and contain some wonderful details of Chesham life. For instance, in July 1591 they buried Hugh Ovyot who was 'slayne by a faule out of a cherrytree'. Then in March 1596 they record, 'Robt Rederidge al Smith sonne of the widoe franklin, wch Robt dyed by cutting of his legg above the knee not lyving one hower after'. An agricultural accident, perhaps — or maybe an amputation which went wrong? I wonder what stories of despair lie behind the numerous suicides. In February 1599 'Jeremie Stanbridg — most fearfully by hanging him selfe ended this p(rese)nt lyfe'. Poor Isbell, the wife of Thomas Bowler of Botley, in July 1600, 'being great wth childe most fearfully by drowning her selfe in a ponde ended this present lyfe'.

The registers also reveal a number of strays, that is,

genealogical missing persons such as:

'Willm makerith of the middle Temple in the Cittie of London gentl(eman) late s(er)vant to myles Sandys of latymersh in the Count. of Buck. esquyer & Elyzabeth daughter of Frances marsh of Luton in the Count. of Bedford gentl(man)'

in the marriage registers, and, in the register of burials for July 1589:

'Moris Lewys of Kynges Langeley in the Count. of hartf(ord) pedlar being slayne in a fraye by an other pedlar comying togeather to this towne on the fayer even was buried.'

I wonder whether some poor family historian is tearing out his hair because he has lost his William in London, or his Elizabeth in Bedfordshire, little knowing that they found their way to Chesham and married just a few days after Christmas in 1602. Perhaps someone else is still searching the Kings Langeley registers in a vain attempt to locate Moris's burial when, all the time, he lies snug in the churchyard at Chesham.

The registers make fascinating reading. Here we see the baptisms of illegitimate children listed as, 'Bridget and Elyzabeth the daughters of Adultery', and 'Edward, sonne of an harlot'. In 1635 they record the burial of '2 Murthered infants'. I wonder what sad story lies behind that stark entry. We can see, too, the tragic results of the Poor Law which condemned the destitute poor to return to their own parish. So often they never reached home: 'August 1579 — buried margarite a poore strang travailling woma(n)'. Their children, too, often died on the way home: 'February 1597 — Jonh up Robert soone of a poore woman trvailling by the high waye'. Many of these burials took place in the winter when the cold and damp took its toll of the sick and undernourished travelling people. The Drayton Beauchamp register, about the same time, records the burial of 'a travilling great bellyd woman'. Poor soul, she was probably being pushed on from parish to parish in spite of her condition, or rather because of it. Each parish would move her on quickly,

before she could give birth and become a liability to their community. Sadly, she never managed to reach her home parish and was buried without anyone even knowing her name.

Chesham took in many nurse children from London, sometimes the unwanted offspring of the well-to-do, or sickly children whose families believed that the country air would be healthier than the plague-ridden air of 17th-century London. The burial registers record their fate. In 1578 'Ric. Smythes wyfe' buried three nurse children, 'margarite a nurse child of London' (March), 'Katherine a nurse child of Ric. Parkes of London' (June), and 'Marc sonne of one hawsefoote of London' (July). The registers reveal the small tragedies in my ancestors' lives, too. Mary, wife of my Peter Batchelor, carried her baby safely for the full nine months only to have him baptised and buried on the day of his birth, 24 June 1632. Even across all those years discoveries like that touch me deeply.

Life was hard in the good old days and the law was harsh. The registers record that 'Jane Gray a vagrant beger was taken beging in this towne of Chesham and was whiped according as the law directs on February ye 12th 1703'. Such rough justice was common throughout England. In London I found reference to a John Tracher who was punished for beating and wounding his master. His punishment was:

'to be whipped in open market on two market days, to serve one day in the stocks, to seek pardon on his knees at the church door, and then to serve one year in prison.'

That would certainly keep other servants and apprentices in their place!

But back to the Chesham registers. After I had spent some time reading the beautifully written documents, George Piggin took me outside to look at the tombstones. Fortunately, some years ago, a travelling salesman with an interest in monumental inscriptions had set himself the task of recording those at St. Mary's whenever he visited the area. Now many of the stones are badly worn and difficult to read, so we must be grateful to him for his painstaking work. As I had expected we found no memorials to my early Batchelors, for their markers were probably wooden and long since rotted away. There were some interesting ones, however. There was George Batchelor who died in May 1839, aged 46. 'He lived servant with Mr. W. Suthery surgeon of this town 28 years'. The stone of 28-year-old John Batchelor of Ashridge, who died in 1851, warned me, 'Take ye heed, watch and pray, for ye know not when the time is'.

A curious thing happened on this first visit to Chesham which should not go unmentioned. I had come armed with my camera to take pictures of my family's church. When I tried to take photographs inside, my flash failed to work, so I ran down into the town for a replacement battery. Now the camera flashed away quite happily as I pointed it at the lovely window dedicated to George's parents, at the striking modern mural of the life of Christ and at various memorials around the walls. I photographed the graves we had found and George himself. Then I asked him to photograph me beside the church door, where the porch is built on two massive pieces of pudding-stone.

When I got home I sent off my two rolls of film and waited in great anticipation for their return. Imagine my incredulity when I opened their envelope to find that on the first film, after the picture of George's window, (which had a strange smearing of light and colour across it) there was nothing at all. The film was a complete blank. The second film was in the same condition, except for the last two exposures. These I had taken from the window of my flat to use up the film. They were perfect. There was no fault in my camera for I used it the next week on my Cornish holiday. How can I explain this? I said jokingly that the ancestors must have been at work, putting the 'mockers' on my research. Strange to say, that is not the only time the inexplicable has happened.

For instance, researching in Luton Library, I switched on a reader and the lense promptly fell out of my reading glasses. 'No you don't,' I muttered to the ancestors, and put on the spare pair which I always carry. I turned back to the reader — and the bulb blew! I know it is really only coincidence, but it's quite fun to pretend that it is THEM again. There was the day I boarded my Rapide coach to London in the pouring rain. Only a few miles up the motorway the driver pulled on to the hard shoulder to wait for a rescue coach because the windscreen wiper in front of him had broken. I was fuming at the delay, for I had to pick up a connecting coach at Marylebone to take me to Mary Geary's, where I was going to stay while I did my research at Hertford. We arrived in London over an hour late and I caught the next coach from Marylebone. I was soon bowling merrily up the M1 towards Bedfordshire. It was still raining. Suddenly the driver pulled over on to the hard shoulder. Once again the windscreen wiper directly in front of the driver had malfunctioned. For the second time that day I found myself waiting for a rescue coach. Coincidence — or ancestors at work?

On another occasion I went to London for the day to research at the Public Record Office. I sat down to read a will, took out my notebook, put on my reading glasses — and the fire alarm sounded. Apparently workmen had cut through the water supply and the regulations don't allow the public to remain in the building without a supply of water in case of a fire. To my great frustration I was told that the office would be closed for the rest of the day. Then there are all those missing documents and registers. 'October 1643 is wanting,' says the note, when that is the very month I want to see. Or, 'Sorry, that register is away being rebound/was lost in a fire in 1620/is being used by the Photocopying Department/is in such a poor condition that it can never be produced.'

When I returned home from my first visit to Chesham my family tree had grown considerably and I had traced my Batchelors back to Thomas of Hawridge who had married his Cecily at Chesham in July 1567. Now, in the post, came a surprise parcel for me. In

Chapel Farm, St. Leonards. © *Antonia Benedek*

Chesham Library George had come across a book about Chiltern villages, including Hawridge, the home of Thomas and Cecily. He rushed to the nearest bookshop and kindly bought me a copy, writing in his note, 'As soon as I saw the index I knew that you must have a copy.' The book was, *Hilltop Villages of the Chilterns*, by David and Joan Hay, and the index listed no fewer than 27 Batchelors in the area between 1468 and 1824. Incidentally, the very day I received my book there was a bomb scare at the Leeds Parcel Office and a warning was given to anyone receiving an unexpected brown paper parcel 'shaped like a book', to inform the police before opening it. Thankfully I had opened my parcel before I read the newspaper, or my lovely Chiltern book might have been blown up by the bomb squad as a suspicious parcel.

On my next visit to Chesham I went armed with *two* cameras, to foil the ancestors. Previously I had left a donation with George to pay for a hassock for St. Mary's in celebration of my parents' golden wedding. Now he took me into the church to try to find the one bearing their name. It was a very satisfying moment when I found it, and nice to think that something from us was now in Chesham church. I told George how delighted I was with my book about 'our' villages. It had contained so much detail about the Batchelors of Hawridge and, earlier, St. Leonards that I had been able to dovetail the top of my family tree into the family revealed by the authors. This now took me back to Andrew Bacheler, who died at Chapel Farm, St. Leonards, in 1527.

I had written to the authors to tell them how much help their book had been, and had received an invitation to visit them. George now took on a new role as my chauffeur and took me, with my friend Mary, to the secluded home of the Hays. They lived in the beautiful Chesham Vale, within sight of Geary's Wood, in a house chock full of books from floor to ceiling. They made us most welcome and told us of their love of the area and its wildlife, including stories of the glisglis (edible dormice) in their attic. Sadly they could tell me little more about my Batchelors, for their book had been written over 20 years before and they had been busy with many other projects since then. However, they signed my copy of *Hilltop Villages*, which now has a special place on my bookshelf, next to my priceless, battered old copy of Garrett Pegge's transcript of the Chesham registers for the years 1538-1636.

Next George took me to visit Tony Harman at Grove Farm. He had just finished filming, for the B.B.C., the story of his life on a Chesham farm, *Seventy Summers*. I spent a fascinating afternoon with him looking up my Batchelors in his volumes of the Buckinghamshire Record Society publications. There I found the record of Robert, my 12xgreat-grandfather, and his brothers William, Thomas, Andrew and Richard, paying a total of £38 tax for the war with the French in 1524. Thomas the younger, my 11xgreat-grandfather, was also listed there paying £5. These were considerable amounts of money over 460 years ago and, as the tax was assessed on income, it was my first intimation that my early Batchelors had been quite well-to-do.

Never satisfied, I now had the urge to visit Chapel Farm, the home of my 13xgreat-grandfather Andrew in 1527. George had told me that it still existed, so one

morning George, Mary Geary and I set off to find my earliest Batchelor home. Somehow I had expected to find a modest farmhouse such as you would see in the Yorkshire Dales. I was not prepared for the grand entrance and long gravel drive which took us through an archway and past the stables to a magnificent timbered house. 'Oh well,' I thought, 'it's worth a try. Too bad if they just tell me to clear off.' Taking a deep breath, I picked up my copy of my family tree (as proof of my story) and with Mary giving me moral support from behind I knocked at the door. A rather surprised lady answered, for unexpected visitors are few and far between at St. Leonards. I explained what I was doing there and asked whether she would mind if I took some photographs of the outside of her house. I was taken aback by her response: 'Do come in. Let me show you round inside, too.'

I had not been prepared for a welcome such as this. With tingling spine I entered the farmhouse where my Andrew had lived so long ago. True, the house had been extended and lovingly restored by generations of owners, including the Allens who live there now, but it is still possible to identify the oldest part of the house with its wattle and daub walls and massive timbers reaching up to the roof. This was the moment I had imagined so long ago, when I had watched Alex Haley's story. This was my village. These were the fields where my people had sweated and laboured. This was my place. Jokingly I asked Joan Allen whether I could re-claim the house, as I was a descendant of Andrew Bacheler, but she would not let me have it.

It was difficult to tear myself away at the end of that first visit, but I have been back many times since and always had the same warm welcome from Joan and Leslie Allen. One of my most memorable visits was when I took my parents there so that my father could see where his ancestors had lived. It was such a satisfying feeling to be able to share this part of my adventure with them. As we took tea in the garden with the Allens, I wondered what Andrew would have made of it all. At least he didn't tamper with my camera!

Chapter Four

Three Dragons for Daniel

'Been putting your hands on history, eh?'
Leeds taxi driver.

Now came the most colourful and thrilling part of my genealogical adventure. It all began when I was spending a day researching at the Society of Genealogists in London. This is a wonderful treasure-house for the family historian. It has libraries on three floors where most of the material is on open access. It is so good to be able to help yourself to such things as transcripts of parish registers, the I.G.I. (Mormon Index), microfilm of actual registers and apprenticeship records. In most record offices and libraries a great deal of time is spent queueing to hand in your request slip and waiting, sometimes for over an hour, for your material to be brought up. Here you can wander at will in an Aladdin's Cave of genealogical material. It is often hot and crowded but that is hardly noticeable in the excitement of the chase. There is a hushed, almost reverent, atmosphere, broken only by the frantic rustle of turning pages and the scribbling of pencils. There is a sense of suppressed eagerness which occasionally gives way to a gasp of delight as someone finds an ancestor. I always enjoy my visits to the Soc. Gen., for I never come away empty-handed.

On this particular afternoon I had gone down my shopping list of records to consult, so I was pottering around rather aimlessly poking my nose into drawers, files and dusty boxes. I came across the Holworthy Collection of Armorial Families and to my great surprise found a coat of arms, bearing three dragons' heads, which had been granted to a Daniel Bacheler of Aston Clinton in 1606 and which had the exciting description, 'gentleman of the Privy Chamber to King James I'. In fact, he proved to be a *Groom* of the Privy Chamber to Anne, the wife of James, but more of that

later. I would not allow myself to claim Daniel as one of my Batchelors without some further proof, though it was very tempting. Could he, I wondered, be the same Daniel who had written a letter on behalf of the Queen, the same year, thanking Robert Cecil for a 'precious cup' which he had sent her? I had collected this reference ages ago, in the Hertford Local Studies Library, hardly believing that he could be one of my family. After all, at this time we were just farming folk in the backwoods of Buckinghamshire, a long way from the royal court. I put this new reference to Daniel Bacheler in my notebook, as one of those odd pieces of my genealogical jigsaw, and awaited developments.

My next school holiday found me once again pottering about at the Society of Genealogists. I am convinced that genealogy is ⅓ skill, ⅓ persistence and ⅓ luck, for all my most exciting discoveries seem to be made by chance and not design. I think the word, serendipity, sums it up: 'The faculty of making happy and unexpected discoveries by accident.' I had found on a shelf some calendars of court documents, so I started at one end of the shelf and worked my way through one volume after another. I always start by looking at the back of such books, where the index of names can be found. In a Calendar of Ancient Deeds I found the entry which linked Daniel of Aston Clinton with my family and also with the royal courts of Elizabeth and James.

What I had found was a reference to a document signing over Daniel's apprenticeship indentures from 'Thomas Cardell, gentleman, servant to our sovereign lady', to no less a person than Sir Francis Walsingham, a rather sinister gentleman who was head of Elizabeth's secret service and her Principal Secretary of State. The document, dated 1586, described the young Daniel as 'son of Richard Batchiler of Aston Clinton'. This was great news, for I already had a Richard of Aston Clinton on my family tree. In his will, which I had in my files, Richard had mentioned his son, Daniel, to whom he left the princely sum of 6s. 8d. This Richard was the great-grandson of Andrew of Chapel Farm. *And* my

Richard was already deceased by the time Daniel's indentures were signed over to Walsingham, which accounts for the fact that his signature is missing. Thomas Cardell and Daniel himself signed it. To confirm further that this was indeed 'my' Daniel, I found that my Richard had been married to Elizabeth Cardell, so Daniel had obviously been apprenticed to some relation of his mother. I guessed that Thomas was his uncle and later I found that I was right.

Now I had to go to the Public Record Office in Chancery Lane, London, to see the original indenture. Security there was very strict. A careful search of my bags by the security guard revealed the travelling genealogist's survival kit — Optrex for bleary eyes, spare reading glasses to foil the ancestors, sandals for hot tired feet and sandwiches for the coach journey home. The amused guard told me where to obtain my Reader's Ticket and I was directed to the impressive Round Room where I was shown how to order the indenture. At that time the P.R.O. used paper application forms which were simple to complete. Now they are modernised and all documents have to be ordered by computer. My first experience with their computer was rather fraught. It kept reprimanding me, telling me there was no such document as the one I had requested. When I finally entered the correct number, it was *very* condescending and remarked, 'Good!' I can't do with machines which answer back. I think I must be a bit of a Luddite at heart.

On that first visit my paper request slip worked perfectly well and a surprisingly small package was delivered to me. Heart pounding, I opened it up and there before me was the original indenture signing Daniel over from his uncle into the household of the Walsinghams. It was extremely detailed, recording the young lad's promise:

Daniel's indenture. PRO E40/12979.

'not to playe at any unlawfull games, not to haunt taverns nor any lewde dyshonest companye nor contracte himselffe in matrymonye to any woman — but in all thinges as an honest, faythfull and diligente apprentyce shall gently, quietly and faythfully use, beare and behave him selfe towarde his said mayster and maysters'.

Sir Francis Walsingham, on his part, promised to:

'gyve, fynde and allowe to his said apprentize meate, drinke, apparell, lynnen, wollen hose, shoes, lodginge, wasshinge and all other things nedefull and necessarie for an apprentise of his degree to have duringe all the terme that the said Danyell shall serve'.

As Daniel had already served seven years of his original 16-year apprenticeship with his Uncle Thomas, this document bound him for a further nine years with Sir Francis and his family. What a great step up the ladder for a young boy. The writing on the document is extremely neat and easy to read. No 'pitchfork dipped in soot' here. I found it difficult to realise that the words were written 400 years ago. My greatest thrill was to see 14-year-old Daniel's own signature, written with great care and precision. After all, this was a legal document taking Daniel into the household of an important and powerful man. The lad had to use his best writing.

Of course, now I had to know what Daniel was doing on the Walsingham payroll. Friends of mine suggested, rather unkindly, that he might have been a spy. After all, it is well-known that Sir Francis had a network of spies to protect the interests of the Queen. However, I found nothing to support this theory, so I concentrated instead on seeking more information on his early life. At Aylesbury I consulted a printed transcript of the Aston Clinton register, but there was no sign of Daniel. I ordered the Bishop's Transcripts, an official copy of the original register, where I searched in vain for the record of Daniel's baptism. As is usually the case, the very years when I estimated his birth could have occured were the years for which the registers appeared to be missing. What frustration! However, as the original indentures were for 16 years, probably ceasing at the age of 24, I estimated that Daniel left home with his Uncle Thomas at the age of eight and was 14 when he joined the Walsinghams in 1586. This would give him a birth date of around 1571/2. When the missing register entry later came to light it confirmed that 'Daniell Bacheller, ye sonn of Ric bacheller bapt March 16 *1571*'. I was chuffed! How nice to be proved right.

By now I was obsessed with finding out more about Daniel. I wrote countless letters — no question of *my* 'postie' being made redundant. I told Duggie they ought to provide him with a bigger sack. Among others I asked the Department of Manuscripts at the British Museum if they had anything referring to my Daniel. Back came their reply, 'No entry in our catalogue for Daniel Bachiler or Bacheler.' I decided, however, to visit them and check for myself. Perhaps he was there under a different spelling.

The wonderful Department of Manuscripts is housed in the same building as the British Museum. The first thing I had to do was to obtain my Reader's Ticket. That may sound straightforward but I reckoned without the intervention of the ancestors. I was asked for proof of identity and I was tempted to simply present my family tree, pointing out my name at the bottom. I resisted the temptation and instead handed over a letter from my Headteacher, Liz Bisson, which assured them that I was a fit and proper person to be trusted with their valuable archive material.

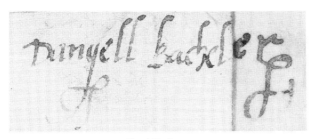

Daniel's signature.

I signed the application form and was then sent to an office to have a photograph taken for my ticket. A sensible security precaution, I thought. 'This will only take a moment,' said the young man cheerfully. Poor soul, he knew nothing of my fiasco with the blank films at Chesham. His camera flashed and we chatted as we waited for the picture to develop. 'Oh dear,' said the young man. 'It's never done *that* before.' 'Have I broken your camera?' I asked. 'Well, someone has,' was the glum reply, and he showed me a completely blank photograph. He had to take me to another camera and this time there was no problem. 'Sorry about that,' he said. 'I can't think what went wrong.' I said nothing. If I had told him my suspicions about the ancestors he might not have thought me a fit and proper person to have a ticket!

Incidentally, the next visit I made was also fraught with problems. I showed my ticket at the desk and ordered the document I had come to see. A few minutes later, an apologetic assistant told me, 'I'm sorry. We can't produce that document for you. It is kept in a locked cabinet and the lock has jammed. As it is Saturday we can't get a locksmith'. I was not going to be thwarted so easily, so I simply ordered a photocopy of the document in question instead. It takes an incredible ten weeks to get a photocopy from the Department of Manuscripts. When, at last, it arrived I couldn't believe my eyes. They had photocopied the wrong document. Foiled again! Ancestors — 2, Anne — nil.

However, on my first visit I was able to look in their card catalogue for Daniel Bachiler or Bacheler. They were quite right. There was no such entry. Not easily satisfied, I looked up all the alternative spellings — and there he was. The card, which was handwritten and not easy to read, said, 'Daniel Bachelor, Galliard for the lute, 1610.' At first I misread this as 'for the late', i.e. deceased, but on looking more closely I saw that it was lute. I wrote my request slip with trembling hand and waited with bated breath. The assistant eventually brought me *Mr. John Sturt's Lute Book*, and it did

indeed contain a galliard composed by Daniel Bachelor. So he was not a spy but a musician. Later I discovered that Sir Francis Walsingham was recognised as a bountiful patron to men of talent. He must have recognised something outstanding in young Daniel's music and so furthered his career by bringing him into his own household.

My next interesting discovery was the name of Thomas Cardell on a list of court musicians as lutenist and dancing master. So Daniel's original apprenticeship was to a man who was able to teach him to play and compose, and who would have taken him into court. I had wondered how Sir Francis came to hear this young lad from a tiny Buckinghamshire village. No doubt he saw and heard him when he came to court with his uncle. Dear old Uncle Thomas was proving to be a key figure in Daniel's story.

I often wonder what made Thomas choose Daniel rather than one of the other sons of Richard Bacheler. Perhaps even at the early age of eight he showed an interest in his uncle's lute? I imagine his parents were happy to let him go to London, where he would no doubt live quite well in his uncle's house. So the little lad came from the farm to the London of Shakespeare and into the court of Gloriana herself. The Westminster City Archives show Thomas Cardell living in Kinges Streete, close to St. Margaret's church where he had married Hellen Cotton in April 1575. In fact, Uncle Thomas has turned up in a great number of court documents. He is listed paying his taxes at Westminster in 1594, 1600 and 1601, where he is variously described as 'one of her Ma(jes)te ordinary musicons', 'one of her Ma(jes)te Lewt Plaiers' and 'one of her hyghnes musicians for the luts'. The P.R.O. has details of the funeral procession of Queen Elizabeth, in which Thomas is listed receiving mourning clothes. They also have his Letters Patent appointing him later to the service of James' wife, Anne of Denmark.

Another surprising entry turned up in those funeral accounts. Whom should I find there but Blackaller — or could it be Blackadder of T.V. fame! Further down the list — I could hardly believe my eyes — was a Baldrick. I had a fit of suppressed giggles but couldn't share my discovery with the solemn-looking folk in the research room. I'm afraid this sort of thing often happens when I am busy researching. I have to be content with a quiet smile to myself when I would really like to chortle out loud. I remember on one occasion, when I was studying an Elizabethan diary, I came across the following, 'We went along with the Queen's train, there being an infinite number of coaches.' I never realised that Queen Elizabeth I travelled by Intercity!

Now I set myself the task of finding some of Daniel's music. Perhaps someone, one day, would play it for me. I met a young student from the Huddersfield Poly. who remarked, 'Daniel Bachiler? Oh yes, we play his compositions at Music College.' I was quite 'took-aback'. Did other people really know my Daniel? Hot on the trail, I plunged into the noisy depths of the huge Virgin Megastore on Oxford Street, to make the amazing discovery that even Julian Bream knew my Daniel and had recorded his *Mounsiers Almaine*. What a wonderful, eerie feeling it was to hear his music for the first time. I was actually hearing what went on inside his head. It made me feel very close to him. Later I discovered that he composed something like 40 pieces for the lute, eight consort pieces (mostly dedicated to the Walsingham family) and one song, a setting of a poem written by the Earl of Essex, husband to the Lady Frances Walsingham. In fact, my Daniel was ranked second only to the great John Dowland, whose son, Robert called him, 'the right perfect' musician.

Some of the Walsingham consort books still survive and I tracked them down to the archives at Hull University. Of course, I then had to trip off to Hull to take a look at them. I had read that there was a distinct possibility that Daniel had been responsible for the music in the Walsingham household and that the books could be in his own hand. I appeared to be the first person to have stumbled upon his indenture, with its personal signature, so I took an enlarged copy with me, to compare with the writing in the books.

With reverent hands I lifted the small books from the box and opened one at random. Now I am no handwriting expert but to my untrained eye there is a great similarity between the two hands. There are two other clues which make me think that Daniel wrote out the music in the books. Wherever composers' names are given at the end of a piece, they are usually given the courtesy title, 'Mr.'. There is Mr. Richard Allison, along with Mr. Richard Jhonson [sic] and Mr. Byrd. However, the pieces by Daniel are always credited to Dan., Daniell or just plain D. Bachiler. Modesty on his part, perhaps? Then there is the list of contents on an unattached page. It is written in the same hand as the music and is headed, 'The note of the Songes in my consorte Bookes'. It gives a list of all the pieces in the books. No one else seems to have noticed an 'x' next to all Daniel Bachiler's pieces and also next to two anonymous items, *Squiers Galliard* and *Primero*. Could it be that I have stumbled upon two undiscovered pieces of Daniel's music? If I have that would be wonderful.

If a handwriting expert is ever able to confirm that the neat signature on the indenture matches the equally neat hand of the Walsingham consort books, then there is one more significant discovery which I made that day at Hull. I felt reluctant to hand back the books to the archivist, because here, without a doubt, were books that my Daniel must have handled. I drooled over them for a while, admiring their olive green calf-skin covers and studying the pages carefully. Suddenly I noticed, on the second page of the flute book, something which stopped me in my tracks. On that page the music of *Sir Francis Walsingham's Goodnight* was written in black ink. At the bottom of the page, in the left hand corner, was an inkblot. In the inkblot was a thumbprint. Could this be my Daniel's own print? If the writing in the book and on the indenture are one and the same, then Daniel wrote the consort books. *If* he wrote the books then he made the blot *and* the thumbprint. I have no proof, of course, but it does seem highly likely and I feel certain within myself. All it needs is for a handwriting expert to offer to compare the two for me. Then I shall know beyond any shadow of doubt. Meanwhile I continue to gather references to Daniel's music. I did come across a note that 'at Eltham (Palace) was heard a consort of music so excellent and sweet as cannot be expressed'. I wonder whether that was some of my Daniel's music?

Two more interesting documents came to light at this point. In August 1599 Queen Elizabeth paid Daniel £10 to carry letters to her beloved Essex, who was in Ireland. This is evidence of great trust on behalf of the Queen, but perhaps Daniel was an obvious choice because of the years he had spent in the Walsingham household. After all, the Lady Francis Walsingham was at that time the wife of Essex. Perhaps Daniel was carrying letters for her, too?

Then I found a curious document signed by Queen Anne, the wife of James I, in 1604 granting to Daniel and his fellow Groom of the Privy Chamber, William Gomeldon, 'a chest of arrows cast up as a wreck in our manor of Portland'. What lies behind this, I wonder? What were two Grooms doing on the beach at Portland? Could they share my hobby of fossil-hunting? Maybe Anne was visiting Portland Castle on a Royal Progress? Was the chest, perhaps, from an Armada wreck? I have yet to discover the full story behind Daniel's chest of soggy arrows. I can't help wondering where they are now!

By this time I had put together an amazing amount of material on my Daniel. All I wanted now, to fill my cup to the brim, was (a) a portrait of him and (b) to find his last resting place. The National Portrait Gallery had never heard of him, nor had the Queen's Gallery at Buckingham Palace. I wrote masses of letters but to no avail. No one had a portrait of him and yet I felt in my bones that there was a picture of him somewhere. The breakthrough came when I found, in *Groves Dictionary of Music and Musicians*, an entry about Daniel which said that a named portrait did exist. It described a picture of Daniel as a young lad riding a warhorse in

Daniel in Sir Philip Sidney's funeral procession, 1587.

(*Reproduced by permission of Viscount De L'Isle, V.C., K.G.*)

Thomas Lant's picture of the funeral procession of Sir Philip Sidney. I was over the moon — until I realised that *Groves* failed to mention where the original picture was to be found. Frustration! I did find a picture from the funeral procession in a library book but, true to form, the book only showed the part of the procession around the coffin. No young lad on a horse.

Now Sir Philip Sidney, who was inside the coffin, had been married to the young Lady Frances Walsingham, so the boy in the procession was, without doubt, my Daniel Bachiler. But where was he? Again I cast numerous letters into the post box and grumbled at my 'postie', Duggie, because he brought me no satisfactory replies. Then I had a brainwave and wrote to Penshurst Place, the home of the Sidney family. This came up trumps. By return of post I received not only confirmation that they had the Lant picture, but also a beautiful photocopy of Daniel, aged by my reckoning about 15, mounted on a horse which was decked out in cloth of gold. Daniel was all dressed up in an enormous hat, and his little feet didn't reach the stirrups. I could imagine the feelings of this young lad from the country as he rode in this grand procession through the streets of London. A far cry indeed from the farm in Aston Clinton. How his life had changed since Uncle Thomas brought him to London only a few years before.

As for his last resting place, this proved to be more difficult. I found reference to the death of a Cecily Bacheler, wife of Daniel, at Twickenham in 1611, but neither of them appeared to be buried there. I got quite excited when I found a Daniel Bachelor buried in St. Margaret Somerset, until I saw the full entry which showed that this Daniel was the infant son of William Bachelor. So I had drawn a blank again, though William does turn up again later. I did find a probate document at the P.R.O. which looked promising. It was a 'sentence', not a will, of 'Daniel Bacheler of Leigh (Kent) gentleman, 1619'. Unfortunately the massive document was in Latin so I had another nail-biting wait for a translation. The sentence proved to be a description of a dispute between William and John,

the natural brothers of gentleman Daniel on the one hand and his nephew, Samuel, on the other. They were arguing about his property, for he died intestate and childless. To me Kent sounded a long way from the royal court, but then I discovered that the Walsinghams had alienated a rectory at Leigh in 1587 so it was quite possible that my Daniel had ended his days there.

I contacted a local historian in Leigh, which is not far from Penshurst, the home of the Sidney family. He insisted that the Walsinghams never had a rectory there. The rectory at Leigh was, he said, a living and not a building. Then, as an afterthought, he added, 'Alternatively there is a village of *Lee* in Kent ... only a few miles from Chiselhurst ... where the Walsingham family resided ... which may have sometimes been spelt Leigh.' Bless him! When I visited the Kent Record Office at Maidstone and asked for the transcript of the parish register of St. Margaret's, Lee, there he was. 'Daniel Bacheler, gentleman, was buried 9th. January 1618/19'. In fact, when I later saw the original register it said, '*vicessmo nono*', that is the *29th*. So you really can't believe the printed word without checking the originals.

Now this Lee, which was spelt Leigh on some of the old maps, did have a rectory and it was only a short journey across Blackheath Common to the royal court at Greenwich. A number of courtiers are known to have lived at Lee because of its proximity to both Greenwich and Eltham Palace. So all the clues pointed to this being my Daniel — but was it? I felt that I needed just one more piece of evidence to convince me. Perhaps there was some record of *my* Daniel's date of death which would fit the Lee burial date? Again old Uncle Thomas Cardell came to my aid.

The evidence came in the wills of Uncle Thomas and his wife, Helen. They both died at Westminster and, in 1617, Thomas had written in his will that he bequeathed 'to my loving nephew Daniel Bacheler esquire my best chaine of gould which I have used to weare'. A gold chain was the time-honoured reward

Lady Frances Sidney née Walsingham.
(Reproduced by permission of Viscount De L'Isle, V.C., K.G.)

Sir Francis Walsingham.

from a monarch to men of eminence and was worn on all public occasions, so Uncle Thomas's bequest to his nephew was something very precious. He also named Daniel later in the will as his 'loving *freind* and nephew', and spoke of 'the truste and confidence which I have' in him. Daniel was responsible for seeing that each of Thomas's daughters received a considerable bequest of £700. I found Thomas Cardell's affection for Daniel very touching. He was obviously proud of his talented nephew. Thomas was brother to Daniel's mother, Elizabeth, as I had guessed. How satisfying to be proved right.

Uncle Thomas's will was not proved until 1621, the year he died. Helen, his widow, made her will in 1624 and in this was the piece of evidence I was seeking. She referred to her husband's arrangements about the

bequests to his daughters. Then, bless her, she said that 'whereas the said Daniel Bacheler *is deceased during the lifetime of my husband*' then other arrangements had to be made. So dear Helen Cardell, in one simple sentence, had given me Daniel's date of death. It had to fall between 1617, when Thomas wrote his will, and 1621 when he died. My entry in the burial register of St. Margaret's, Lee, in 1618/19 fell beautifully into that time slot. I now went hot-foot to search for Daniel's church at Lee.

I hardly dared to believe it would still be there after all these years. After all, it could have been turned into a carpet warehouse or mosque, as has happened to many churches in the industrial north. Perhaps it had been demolished and now lay under Tesco's or a multi-storey car park. To my delight the kind lady at Lee

Portrait of Anne of Denmark.

Green Post Office told me that there was a St. Margaret's church, still in use, and directed me to it. Of course, in my excitement and in pouring rain, I got lost and appealed for help at an official looking building. This proved to be the Blackheath College of Music, quite appropriate as I was seeking my musical Daniel. They pointed me in the right direction but warned me that St. Margaret's was a Victorian church.

Rather troubled in spirit now, I ploughed on through the rain. What kind of fool am I, I asked myself, to come all the way from Yorkshire on such a wild goose chase? Eventually I found the Victorian church of St. Margaret. Perhaps it might contain something from the

old church — a coat of arms, or maybe some reference to Daniel? I knocked at the Rectory door, only to be told that the Rector had gone out for the day with the children. His housekeeper, though sympathetic, did not have the authority to let me look in the locked church. I felt completely deflated, standing there with the rain dripping off my hair and running off the end of my nose. In a sad voice I told her why I had wanted to visit the church. 'Oh,' she said. 'You want the *old* church! It's that ruined tower you can see over the road.' And so it was. I could hardly believe my eyes. Daniel's church had survived as an ivy-clad ruin surrounded by old tombstones.

There was no way I could identify Daniel's exact burial spot, for the wooden marker on his grave would have rotted away centuries ago, but just to know that he was buried there was enough. It was a very moving experience, having followed the fortunes of this young musician from his humble beginnings as a farmer's son, through the colourful courts of Elizabeth and Anne, to this deserted churchyard. I sat on the wall and, in my head, sang the melody of his *Mounsiers Almaine*. It was good to think that after all those years of neglect, at last, someone had visited his last resting place and remembered him. I have now stood in the only two places where I know for certain that Daniel has been. I have stood in the church where he was carried to his baptism and in the churchyard where he was carried for burial.

Having found his place, I felt that I wanted to leave something tangible as I had done for old Theophilus in the cemetery at York. I went to a flower shop in nearby Blackheath and asked the girl for a single red rose. 'Is it for someone special?' she asked with a smile. 'Yes,' I said. 'It's for a man who died over 360 years ago.' She looked at me blankly for a moment and then said, 'Oh, we don't get much call for that sort of thing.' I returned to the churchyard, found a picturesque ivy-covered tomb and placed Daniel's rose there. It was my personal tribute to my 'right perfect musicon'.

Feeling emotionally drained by all the day's exciting

experiences, I took a long walk down into Lewisham. Taking my tea in the Pizza Hut I had a secret giggle to myself. Pop music was coming from the speaker on the wall beside me. I caught the words, 'I still haven't found what I'm looking for'. I wanted to stand on my table and tell everyone, 'But *I* have!'

Of course, now I was greedy for more details of Daniel's life. I wanted to know about his role in the court of Anne of Denmark. What *was* a Groom of the Privy Chamber? I asked the staff at the Public Record Office and was advised to write to Dr. David Starkey of the London School of Economics. Apparently he had just written a book about the royal courts. That suggestion was to put me in contact with a researcher who was to become one of my most important 'postal friends'. He was to help me find more references to Daniel in the court records than I could ever have found unaided. My letter to Dr. Starkey, which followed him to America, brought a reply which told me that the chapter on the courts of James and Anne had been written by a Neil Cuddy who was now in Canada.

Hot on the trail once more, I wrote an air-letter to him, explaining my interest. Back came the first of many extremely helpful letters containing not only a description of Daniel's position and duties but also the catalogue numbers of some documents which actually contained references to him. It was a wonderful feeling to come across someone who already knew of my Daniel. Neil told me that originally Grooms were responsible for cleaning and making ready the Privy Chamber and were expected to run errands and carry messages. However, by the time Daniel was in court the Grooms were no longer expected to perform such menial duties. Neil wrote, 'Certainly the presence of Samuel Daniel, the poet and dramatist, John Florio, the dictionarist and Italian scholar, and John Maria, the musician among the Grooms' number suggests that the position carried status, often filled by those with special talents.'

With Neil's help I was able to see the record of Daniel's annual salary, which included payment for livery. I then found for myself what a Groom's livery would have been:

> 'One gowne of Damaske or Satten garded with velvit and furred with budge (i.e. lambskin worn with the wool outwards)
> one coate of velvit
> one dublet of velvit
> one coate of Marblecloth garded with velvit
> and one other coate of green clothe gded wth velvit'.

It sounds quite splendid. Daniel became the highest paid Groom of Anne's Privy Chamber. In 1616 he received a massive £160 p.a. whereas the other six Grooms were paid between £60 and £100 each. The salary for an ordinary lutenist ranged from £20 to £40 p.a., so my Daniel must have been quite well-to-do.

Neil's letters to me usually contained phrases such as, 'You might find something useful in E351.' He was always right, though E351 could run to over a hundred folios, or pages, all in Secretary Hand. Each page was enormous and joined to its fellows across the top so the document had to be laid along the reading table. This made the lines of writing run in a vertical direction rather than horizontal. To read it I had to tilt my head over to one side. Ignoring the fascinating references to 'Her Majesty's Rat-catcher and Moletaker', I eventually found a payment to Daniel on the forty-third page. By this time my neck had set in its tilted position, with my right ear resting on my shoulder. As I tried to straighten up and unkink my spine I felt like Quasimodo. Perhaps, I thought, Elizabethans wore ruffs to disguise their surgical collars!

I am deeply indebted to Neil for his invaluable help and continued interest in my research. I was able to tell him so in person when we met for a brief half hour in the Members' Room at the P.R.O. where, over a cup of coffee from the machine, we both chattered away about our obsessions. It was a strange and wonderful experience to talk with someone who was so immersed in the life of the courts. Neil spoke of Sir Francis

Walsingham, Robert Cecil and Anne of Denmark as though he knew them personally. How lovely, too, to talk to someone who understood my obsessive quest for Daniel. Our meeting was all too brief, but you don't waste precious researching time talking too long. So we parted, Neil to continue his research for his next book, on Robert Cecil, and I following up references to Daniel in court records. I found the official Heralds' Visitation records which showed Daniel's grant of arms in 1606, where he was described as, 'of Aston Clinton and of the Privy Chamber'. In the same year he was sent by Anne to pay £5 to Robert Henlake 'for mendinge her ma(jes)ties Vyalls (and) Lutes'. Trawling through these old records is time-consuming and often wearisome work, but all that is forgotten in that wonderful moment when the name 'Bacheler' leaps off the page, and I go home boggle-eyed but with a broad grin like the cat that got the cream.

I tried to immerse myself in the period by reading anything set in Daniel's time. In Lytton Strachey's book *Elizabeth and Essex*, I found a reference which gave me a few anxious weeks. He mentioned 'a certain Daniel' who stole and forged letters belonging to Lady Frances, wife of the Earl of Essex. She was Walsingham's daughter. I read on, with mounting horror, as the story told how this Daniel had his ears nailed to the pillory and was then given life imprisonment. Surely this was not my Daniel? I hunted for some reference in Strachey's book but he never revealed where he found this story. Eventually, at the Soc. Gen., I tracked down the records of the Star Chamber. There was a detailed account of the trial.

'17 Junij, Ano. Doni. 1601.

The Earl of Essexe being ... a prisoner at the Lord Keeper's house and the Countess ... being then in child-bed at Walsingham House, she delivered a rich caskette of letters to one of her women, ... Reona, ... married to ... John Daniel, to the intent that the said woman would keep it secret and safe, containing very many letters of love and passion and kindness ... between the Earl and his wife ... then

the said John Daniel one morning looking for his slippers, tossed and tumbled the bed in his house ... and under the boulster found this rich casket ... took twenty or thirty of the letters ... and ... carried them to Peter Bales, a notary ... to Copye ... .'

So, thankfully, the miscreant was *John* Daniel. I was so relieved. The thought of my lovely musician having his ears pierced in this barbaric and painful fashion distressed me dreadfully. I breathed again.

Now I became interested in performances of early music, trying to soak up something of the atmosphere of Daniel's time. I went to numerous concerts by local groups such as Estampie, Fairfax and the York Waites. I went to hear Anthony Rooley, the talented lutenist, many times, watching avidly as his fingers flew across the strings. This was my Daniel's instrument and I tried to visualise him as a young lad, providing a kind of musical wallpaper in the Walsingham home and, later, in the Queen's Privy Chamber as she met with her friends and her statesmen.

Sadly, no one seemed to play Daniel's music. When I asked why, I was told that it is very complex and difficult to play. Most early music concerts feature the lute music of John Dowland, a contemporary of Daniel Bacheler. 'Blessed John Dowland again!' I mutter to myself as I scan yet another printed programme looking for Daniel's name. It may sound like a beatification or a benediction but it is sheer frustration. I had a wry smile to myself when I discovered that John Dowland said of himself, '*Semper Dowland, semper dolens*' — 'Always Dowland, always dismal'. Early music concerts certainly are 'Semper Dowland' and seldom Daniel.

Then, out of the blue, two lovely things happened. I went to an early music concert held in the atmospheric surroundings of St. Michael le Belfry as part of the York Early Music Festival. There I heard my first live performance of Daniel's music. A young lady, Lynda Sayce, played a lute solo, and another member of the group sang Daniel's only surviving song, *To plead my faith*. I was over the moon. Things were looking up.

Next Peter Bull, of Estampie, suggested that it might be a good idea for me to get in touch with his lute tutor, Martin Eastwell, who had studied the historical setting of lute music as well as being a teacher of original technique. So I had the first of many fascinating telephone conversations with Martin, the man I came to regard as my personal lutenist. I don't know who was the more excited during that first conversation. I was so thrilled to talk to someone who not only knew and admired my Daniel and his music, but also someone who could tell me a great deal about Daniel's actual technique. I absolutely glowed with pride when Martin told me what a remarkable and talented musician Daniel was. Forgetting I was on the telephone, I grinned with delight and waved my arms about in extravagant gestures as I described my search for Daniel and my excitement at my discoveries. Martin was equally enthusiastic, saying how wonderful it was to hear so much new information about one of his favourite musicians.

Gradually I began to realise that the research I had done for my own pleasure and satisfaction was, in fact, of great importance and was stirring up a great deal of interest in the musical world. None of the reference books I have consulted showed any detailed information on Daniel Bacheler. They said vague things like, 'Born ?c1574, died after 1610', or 'His biography remains almost a complete blank', or, 'Very little is known about this musician'. Had I got news for them! I now had a massive file, two inches thick, of photocopied documents relating to Daniel, as well as a heap of other material in envelope files stacked on a shelf in my flat. 'Very little is known', my hat!

I was often on the telephone to Martin with questions about the kind of lute Daniel would have played or the possible dating of some piece. He was extremely patient with my total ignorance of things musical, and very eager to help. Then, one day, he suggested that he might call to see me on his way north to visit his family. Would I like him to bring his lute and play me some of Daniel's music? What a question! He arrived carrying

the oddly shaped lute case which opened to reveal a most beautiful instrument. When I picked it up, very gingerly, I was amazed at the way it almost floated out of my hands. It was like holding eggshell. The pictures I had seen had not prepared me for the great delicacy and fragility of the lute. I put it down quickly, fearful that I might drop it. Then Martin began to play. This was one of those moments I shall treasure. I sat entranced, like a queen with her own personal lutenist, as Martin gave me a private recital of some of my Daniel's music. It was pure magic.

Since that day I have been to several of Martin's concerts and to lute workshops he has tutored in the

My personal lutenist, Martin Eastwell.

lovely setting of Fountains Hall, an Elizabethan house less than an hour's drive from my home in Leeds. It has been fascinating to watch lutenists learning their craft. I had never realised how hard one must work at mastering the lute and perfecting technique. What a clever lad my Daniel must have been to learn at such an early age. And what a skilful musician he must have been himself, to write music of such complexity that modern lutenists find it difficult to play.

Between them, Neil and Martin helped me to put flesh on the bones of my Daniel. He is to me now not merely an interesting character from my family's past but a person I feel I know really well. As for the rest of his story, there are still small gaps which frustrate me. For example, was Cecily really his wife? If she was, wherever did they marry? I have found no record of their marriage at either Hampton or Twickenham, both places named in connection with her probate document when she died in 1611. I have combed the records of London churches and lists of marriage licences, but to no avail. Perhaps a clue lies in John Chamberlain's letter to Dudley Carleton in 1608:

'The young Lord Cranbourne was maried the first of this moneth very privately at the lady Walsingham's lodging by the Tilt Yard: which me thinckes was not so fit, for holy things shold be solemnised in holy places.'

It is believed, too, that my 'blessed' John Dowland's marriage was declared before witnesses in a private house and not solemnised in a church. Perhaps Daniel's marriage, too, was a private affair? Certainly when he died in 1618/19 he left no widow, so he either lost his wife earlier, or he was a bachelor Bacheler. One day perhaps all will be revealed.

The other detail I should like to have is an official record of how he died. My mother's theory is that he was mugged on his way home from the palace at Greenwich. To get home to Lee he would have to cross the notorious Blackheath Common, a dangerous place at night for a solitary traveller. She could be right. My favourite explanation, my own theory, is that he died as a result of a fire which destroyed the Banqueting-house at Whitehall in January 1618/19. Could Daniel have rushed into the flames to save his lute and died from burns or smoke inhalation? He was buried only 13 days after the fire. John Chamberlain said that 'some are hurt and maymed.' Could Daniel have been one of them?

Of course, the most likely explanation is not nearly so romantic. From the beginning of December 1618 until late February 1618/19, smallpox raged through London and infected many courtiers. According to an eye-witness:

3 December 'the small pockes … are so generally spread that yt is verely thought every third house in this towne hath ben infected with them'.

12 December 'the furie of the small pockes is not whit abated … here died 215'.

3rd January 'Sir John Smith is arrested by the small pockes. That disease hath likewise seased on Sir Charles Howod's lady'.

He goes on to say that:

'Lord Mordant and Lady Lile lie very sick of them and yf this cold weather do not coole and abate theyre furie God knows how we shall do in summer'.

So perhaps my lovely musician's face was ravaged by smallpox. What a sad thought. I wonder whether his lute was buried with him?

A curious sight was seen over London that winter. 'A mighty blazing comet' was seen on 18 November and 11 December. It was said that 'these apparitions do always portent some horrid Events here Below', and the comet was thought to have foretold the death of the queen, Anne of Denmark, who died in March. Of course, we know the 'horrid Event' it really foretold. That was the imminent death of a remarkable man who rose from his humble beginnings in a Buckinghamshire farmhouse to a place of honour in the royal court, where he was recognised as 'the right perfect musicon, Daniel Bacheler'.

Chapter Five

The Timewatch Experience

*'There were some wonderful moments in it which
were quite magic.'*
Pat Turley (B.B.C. cameraman).

I was in the Long Gallery at Penshurst Place, Kent. Beside me sat Viscount De L'Isle, a descendant of the Elizabethan Sidney family. Jakob Lindberg, considered by many to be the leading lutenist of our time, was playing my favourite piece of Daniel's music — for me. Around us was a confusion of sound recordists, lighting engineers, camera crew and a B.B.C. production team. I found myself thinking, 'Is this really happening — or am I dreaming?' It was no dream. That day at Penshurst was the exciting culmination of my search for Daniel.

As I have already said, I never went looking for anyone famous in my family, so my discovery of him had been purely accidental. However, having found him I felt driven to share my discovery with anyone who would listen. I bored both family and friends with him and sent articles to various genealogical magazines. Then, as I watched television one night in 1988, I began to wonder whether the B.B.C. would be interested. I wrote to the series editor of the history programme, *Timewatch*, telling him the story of Daniel's life and suggesting that it would make an interesting biographical item for the programme. I said that I thought it would make colourful television, for actors in costume could tell his story and musicians could play his music on early instruments. The B.B.C. thanked me for my suggestion and said that it would be considered at their planning meeting in the autumn.

Autumn came and went and I heard no more, so I shrugged my shoulders philosophically and pressed on with my quest for the Batchelor family. Just before Christmas, quite out of the blue, I had a telephone call

from a *Timewatch* producer, Antonia Benedek, who asked whether she could come to Leeds to discuss my suggestion further. As I waited for her at the ticket barrier at Leeds City Station, I must admit that I felt apprehensive. What sort of person would a T.V. producer be? Would I find her intimidating? Would I have to work very hard to convince her of Daniel's suitability for a *Timewatch* programme?

I need not have worried. Antonia was a soft-spoken lady with a gentle smile. She was highly skilled at getting to the 'nitty-gritty' of a conversation and drawing out of me what she wanted to know. I soon felt at ease with her and, at my flat, showed her my incredible hoard of Daniel-material. Then she dropped her bombshell. 'This is wonderful,' she enthused, 'but what we would really like to tell is *not* Daniel's story but yours. It would be far more interesting to the viewers to hear how you found him.' I had not bargained for this. What had I let myself in for? I was stunned but heard myself agreeing with her. What a very persuasive lady she was.

Antonia returned to Elstree Studios to try to convince the series editor, Roy Davies, that my story would make good television. Amazingly he agreed, but insisted that we should also include the story of all my family research prior to Daniel, starting with Grandma Batchelor's family Bible. So it was that in January 1989 Antonia and I did a 'recce' of locations in Leeds and York, during which I gave her a new experience — transport in my faithful, 15-year-old Reliant Robin, TUB 45M. I understand from a business meeting I once attended that 'you are what you drive'. I guess that this makes me a true eccentric, for TUB and I have done a great deal of genealogical travelling together. We have been to cemeteries and libraries, to streets that are not there any more, to visit surviving Batchelors and to Early Music Festivals. Antonia pronounced the experience, 'Fun!', and went back to Elstree to make plans for our programme.

During the next few weeks we met several times to chew things over, and almost before I had chance to develop cold feet, the film crew were arriving at my flat for the preliminary meeting prior to the first day's filming. Antonia introduced me to her assistant, another Ann, an extremely efficient young woman with a cool and level-headed approach to her very demanding work. She had a rather interesting bump up front. Her unborn first child accompanied us throughout my *Timewatch* adventure, increasing in size as filming progressed. When, some months later, her little boy was born I was quite disappointed to learn that he was not going to be called Daniel, but then I can hardly expect everyone to share my obsession.

The cameraman was Pat, a real professional, who, with great skill, managed to charm a good performance out of me and also initiated this absolute ignoramus into the mysteries of television. His camera work was superb and the success of my programme was due in no small way to his talent behind the camera. His assistant was Sheila. I knew we would get on well as soon as I saw her 'Save the Whales' sweater. She was Pat's right hand. Bill was the sound man, whose calm and quiet manner helped settle any nerves I might have had. He was very understanding and put me at my ease, after we had done three 'takes' of a sequence, by telling me that Mr. X (a very famous star of stage and T.V.) had the previous week done 27 'takes' to get one scene right. Bill's microphone, fur-covered to muffle the sound of the wind, became known as 'the hamster'. He made an interesting point that no one notices a sound man's work on a programme unless it goes wrong.

These five people made up the crew who were to work closely with me over the next couple of months. Several different lighting technicians were used during filming. I must pay tribute to them, too, for had they not done their job well the film would not have been the undoubted success it was. I had been warned by a friend that the B.B.C. team would take over my flat completely and how right she was. 'We don't want all these flowers', said Antonia, sweeping them away into another room. 'We'll have the armchair here and —' thus she reorganised my home without a by your leave.

However, she knew what she was doing, for the result was just right.

The next morning we began in earnest. I had insisted that two people at the Leeds end of my adventure must be included in my film — Audrey and her taxi, and Duggie, my postie, with his bag of exciting letters. Audrey had never once let me down in the five years I have been chasing my ancestors, always getting me to my coach or train in time. Duggie, who has been my postman for as long as I can remember, delivers letters safely to me no matter how weird the spelling of my address. He often hands them over to me with a brief weather report. 'Watch the roads this morning. It's very icy out there', or, 'Lovely and sunny today.' I did want to include his smiling face in my programme, and Antonia agreed.

She wanted the first sequence to show me leaving my home and setting off on my travels. The idea was to start filming at 6.15am, when it would still be dark. I would be seen at my lighted window, near the top of my high rise block, waiting for Audrey. This would look quite dramatic, we thought. I was at my place by the window just after 6am but the crew decided to go off to film elsewhere on the estate first. By the time they came back it was broad daylight and a rather worried Audrey, plus taxi, was wondering whether she had come on the wrong morning.

Eventually we started filming. Ann and I went down in the lift together. She was in touch with Antonia by 'walkie-talkie' and probably woke up half the residents in the flats as Antonia's voice echoed around the entrance hall and lift. I'm sure they must have thought it was a police raid. Next I was to walk to Audrey's waiting taxi and put my travelbag in the boot. As this was 'only pretend' I had not bothered to actually pack my bag, but I didn't want to carry what was obviously an empty piece of luggage, so I put in my padded anorak for bulk and a selection of my fossils for weight. As Pat had told me, television is all illusion. I handed my bag over with the usual, 'Morning, Audrey.' Then I tried to get into her taxi, only to find the door locked.

We filmed this sequence again — and again — and again. I was now learning that one take was seldom enough. The same action had to be repeated several times so that I could be filmed from a number of different angles. Now, over a year later, I still can't hand over my luggage to Audrey without a grin and a sly look over my shoulder for the camera.

We now adjourned to my home where the seven of us had breakfast — no mean feat in a small, one-bedroomed flat. Later Duggie arrived and we filmed the delivery of some exciting large brown envelopes from the P.R.O. and the Buckinghamshire Record Office. I was filmed talking about how I came to have the family Bible and about my early discoveries about George and Eliza and old Theophilus. Luckily I have never been camera-shy so this was not too much of an ordeal. Antonia sat beside the camera and I simply told my story to her, as she smiled and nodded at me like one of those little dogs you see in the backs of cars.

The next morning Audrey picked me up at 5.30am and took me to the coach station in Wellington Street, where I was to be filmed boarding the Rapide coach to London. Again I took along my bag of fossils. It was a bitterly cold morning in late February and we seemed to spend a great deal of time just 'stood standing' before anything actually happened. Then the local manager arrived and gave us an empty double-decker coach of our very own to play with. A number of people innocently awaiting the arrival of their own coach were herded towards our coach and persuaded to pretend to board it. We then released them, twittering among themselves in excitement at the prospect of being on the telly. However, we still had a problem, for I could hardly be seen driving off to London in an empty coach. Then the manager had a brainwave. He rushed across the road to his office and asked the surprised staff, 'Who would like to be on television?' We soon had plenty of volunteers.

Next some time was spent filming in City Square and on the motorway, from which I watched with glazed eyes as the high rise offices of Leeds receded into the distance like a North Country version of Dallas. I had been up at 4am and was beginning to feel weary. By now it was only 9.45am and we still had a great deal to do that day. We had a late breakfast, then picked up my parents and carried them off to York to film a couple of sequences there. We filmed outside the house in All Saints Lane, where Grandma Batchelor was born and from which she crossed the narrow pavement to All Saints Church as a young bride.

Neither of my parents can walk unaided, so I had one on each arm as we travelled, 'dignified and stately', along the narrow lane. After one take my father said, 'That's it, then?' and was amazed that we had to do the same thing several times. Thankfully it was a bright, sunny day, though very cold. We had started off walking quite briskly but each take saw us walking slower. We crossed North Street and filmed a beautiful sequence looking across the river towards the Guildhall. Antonia encouraged my father and mother to talk about their childhood in York, but sadly this delightful sequence was never used in the finished film. Finally we filmed at Bootham Bar, within sight of the Minster, before adjourning to a nearby cafe where my father tucked into a double helping of hot bacon sandwich, courtesy of the B.B.C., as a reward for all his hard work.

No rest for the wicked, they say, so the next morning saw me travelling from Leeds to Hertford, this time with real clothes in my bag in place of the fossils. There I had about 20 minutes to recover from the journey before I was once again in front of Pat's camera. We were in the Hertfordshire Record Office, filming my discovery of George and Eliza in the North Church parish records. When I had originally found them it was on microfilm of the marriage register for, in order to preserve them, original registers are seldom produced. However, such is the power of the B.B.C., this time I was allowed to see the actual register in which my George and Eliza put their mark on their marriage day. It was a moving moment.

Then I had to explain to camera what this entry was

and how significant it was to me. I was not allowed to use any notes or memory cards, so I had carefully planned in my mind exactly what I wanted to say. Just before the camera rolled Antonia added, 'And don't forget to mention Joseph the gardener and why this discovery was important. Are you ready? Action!' Hastily I had to rethink what I was going to say, adding the piece about Joseph. Antonia always told me that, if necessary, we could always break up the longer sequences into short bursts, but I always tried to keep going and do a complete sequence without a break. Antonia told me, when we had completed the programme, that she was aware of driving me hard but she had every confidence that I could cope.

Timing was crucial and I had to aim for a talking speed of three words per second, which left no time for pausing for thought. The whole sequence at Hertford was to be 40 seconds long. In that time I had to say where I was, what I was looking for, explain the marriage entry of George and Eliza, pointing out that they could not write their names, explain that George's father was not given as old Theophilus but Joseph the gardener, give George's relationship to Theophilus, describe why Theophilus came to York and encouraged George and Eliza to do the same, and finally explain why the discovery of Joseph the gardener was so important to me. Forty seconds to say all that. No wonder I felt under pressure.

The most difficult thing was not remembering what to say but my exact words and gestures as I said it. The sequence was filmed several times from different angles or at different distances and at each take I had to try to use exactly the same words and movements of the hands. Our eagle-eyed production assistant, Ann, would soon tell me if I removed my reading glasses with a different hand or gestured towards the register at a different point in the sequence. No wonder that by the sixth take my eyes can be seen to be blearing over.

Another thing that I had to keep in mind was the fact that other people were actually researching in the same room, so I felt obliged to try to keep my voice down. I

developed a hushed voice similar to that of David Attenborough in his famous sequence with a family of wild gorillas breathing down his neck. It was a loud whisper with a hint of supressed excitement. My only fear was that the excitement would be totally supressed by sheer weariness. After all, I had now been travelling and filming, with very intense concentration, for three solid days. There was yet more to come the following day, but what a special delight that was going to be.

The next morning found me at Woodford Green in Essex. We were filming at the home of Robert Spencer, a lutenist, singer and specialist in Early Music. Again I had the wonderful experience of meeting someone who knew my Daniel. Apparently he had been researching Daniel for a number of years himself, but I had the advantage of knowing Daniel's family before I discovered Daniel. Researching him via his family, and in particular with the help of his uncle, Thomas Cardell, I had been able to put together his story from the cradle to the grave, something which a more academic study could not have revealed.

To my intense frustration, every time Robert and I began to chatter together about Daniel, Antonia would separate us saying, 'Save that for later.' I don't want you

With Early Music expert, Robert Spencer.

53

to talk together until the camera is on you.' I saw her point, but I was itching to ask Robert so many questions. At long last everything was ready and filming began. Robert and I talked together about Daniel's early life and I shared with him my excitement at discovering the indenture and the portrait at Penshurst. Then it was Robert's turn to astonish me. I had always wondered where Daniel had gone after the death of Sir Francis Walsingham. The years between the death of Sir Francis in 1590 and Daniel's appearance in the court of Anne of Denmark in 1603 were a complete blank. Robert now provided me with some missing pieces of Daniel's biographical jigsaw. He pointed out that Daniel's indentures were to Sir Francis and his *heirs*, that is, to the whole family. Therefore Daniel would have remained with them when Sir Francis died. The widowed Lady Sidney, Walsingham's daughter, then married Robert Devereux, the dashing, handsome, headstrong Earl of Essex, favourite of Queen Elizabeth. It appears that Daniel went with her into the household of the Earl, for Robert was able to show me a copy of the Devereux accounts which mention Daniel. In 1595, when he had almost reached the end of his apprenticeship, Daniel was paid a salary of £7. 10s. per quarter.

It now became clear to me that the Lady Frances was a key figure in Daniel's rise to fame, for Robert explained to me how Daniel came to court and to the attention of the Queen. When James and Anne came from Scotland to claim the throne of England in 1603, their son, Prince Henry, was nine years old. John Chamberlain's letter tells how the King commanded the newly married Lady Frances to bring her son, the twelve year old Robert, to court to be companion to the young prince. She obviously brought with her the members of her household, including Daniel. No doubt the Queen heard him play and, being a great patron of the arts, decided to give him a place at court. Robert sang Daniel's only surviving song for me, his setting of Robert Devereux's poem. He explained to me that the Earl of Essex was in the habit of making his complaints to Queen Elizabeth in the form of a song, and that Daniel may well have set several poems to music for him. Only this one has survived. Robert sang it beautifully and with great feeling, accompanying himself on the lute. Sadly, this was not included in the finished film due to lack of time.

It was Robert Spencer who gave me the title for my film and also for this book. The B.B.C. had given it the working title of *A Batchelor's Life*, which I didn't like at all. Robert suggested *The Batchelor's Delight*. This was the title of a piece of music by Daniel's contemporary, Richard Allison. I had already come across this music, which many people believe was dedicated to my Daniel by the composer. I changed the title slightly to read *A Batchelor's Delight* because I am A. Batchelor and both film and book are about the delight I have experienced researching my family. I could have happily spent all day talking with this very knowledgeable man but we had to get on with filming. I wanted to say to the film crew, 'Just go away and come back tomorrow, will you, please?' Perhaps one day I shall get a chance to sit down and talk Daniel with Robert on my own.

By now I felt that I was being swept along at an increasing speed. We were over half way through our schedule and had only four more days' filming to do. One thing I noticed that made me smile was the very great care Antonia took of me whenever I crossed a road. After all, it wouldn't do for me to break an arm or leg at this point in the proceedings. As our filming was done out of sequence it would have been difficult to explain a broken arm in the first ten minutes of the film which disappeared for a quarter of an hour, only to re-appear in the closing sequence. I became aware that I was a rather valuable piece of B.B.C. property. It was a nice feeling.

After the weekend came a day filming in London. What a revelation that was. I had always imagined that a group of people filming in the street would generate a great deal of public interest, but in London no one seemed to notice. Had we set up our camera in the centre of Leeds I'm sure that a small crowd would soon

In front of the TV camera. Photograph courtesy of Kent and Sussex Courier.

have gathered. Perhaps people in London are more blasé about the media. We filmed first in the wonderful library at the Society of Genealogists in Charterhouse Buildings. It was actually Monday, the day the library is closed to the public. It was quite eerie to see so many empty chairs when I was used to having to hunt for a seat. There was an unearthly silence, too, instead of the frantic scrabbling of papers and scribbling of pencils.

It was here that Sheila, the cameraman's assistant, taught me the usefulness of elephants. Antonia wanted me to wait behind a bookcase until I heard the call, 'Action!' I was then to count to five before walking into view and taking a book from a shelf. This presented a problem, for I obviously counted faster than I should. After a couple of false starts due to my appearing too

soon, Sheila took me aside and whispered to me, 'It's a good idea to count *elephants* — one elephant, two elephants, three elephants —. You will probably find that the timing is just right then.' She was right, too. I stood out of sight of the camera and, like an idiot, muttered, 'One elephant, two elephants —,' ending for good measure with, 'and a baby one at the end of the line.' Then I stepped out and we completed the shot to the great satisfaction of all present.

After a long session filming there we pressed on to Oxford Street, where we had permission to film my visit to Virgin Records in search of Daniel's music. This proved to be quite hilarious. Pat set up his camera on the pavement near the entrance and asked me to walk towards it, and then turn and enter the store.

'Don't look at the camera at all,' he said, 'but always keep within sight of it.' Not an easy thing to do on a crowded pavement, believe me.

I walked towards the camera, turned and entered the store, only to discover to my horror that I was on a one-way escalator being carried down into the bowels of the building. It was not possible to turn and come out again to ask whether the shot was satisfactory. I was carried down into a whirlpool of flashing lights and loud music. I had to weave my way through crowds of young people, find a staircase, go up to the ground floor and find the Oxford Street exit. There I was met by an anxious Antonia who probably thought that she had lost me for good. The crew were waiting to take another shot at it because a crowd of tourists had got between me and the camera.

We repeated the shot, along the street, in at the entrance, down the escalator, along the basement level, up the stairs, through the store and out, past an increasingly suspicious security guard. When I passed him for the fifth time he began speaking into his walkie-talkie, and I expected, at any moment, to feel a hand on my shoulder as he apprehended me for highly suspicious behaviour. I took the bull by the horns. 'You must be wondering why I keep coming in and out,' I remarked with what I hoped was a disarming smile. 'You see, we are making a television film.' I nodded towards the crew and camera. 'Oh, is that all?' he said, and turned away, muttering something unintelligible into his walkie-talkie. I think he was probably calling off the S.A.S.

We filmed inside Virgin Records, too, and were almost completely ignored by the customers, who were far too busy hunting their music to be bothered with us. I did hear one girl ask her friend, 'Who *is* she?' I wanted to say, 'It's Anne Batchelor from Leeds having an unbelievable adventure,' but before I could, her friend had shrugged her shoulders and they moved on. We moved on, too, to the stairs leading to Chancery Lane Underground Station. Here I witnessed the power of the B.B.C. Antonia, unaided, simply stopped a great crowd of people who were surging up the steps by barring their way and declaring, 'Stop! You can't go up yet.' She reminded me of the man who, on the war-time radio programme, *In Town Tonight*, used to halt the roar of London's traffic in a similar way. Curiously, no one questioned the authority of this slight figure with her outstretched arms and woolly hat. So Pat was able to film me as I staggered up the steps several times, on weary feet.

Then it was down Chancery Lane to the beautiful wedding-cake of a building which is the Public Record Office. It seemed strange not calling for my usual super sandwich and piece of pecan pie, which I always pick up on my way to the P.R.O. I am a great believer in fortifying the inner woman before embarking on a day's research, especially if I had my breakfast in Leeds at 4.30am. My special sandwich and pecan pie are one of this Batchelor's delights. I remember, on my first visit, asking the security guard on the gate where I could get something to eat. He advised me to walk up the lane and look for a queue of legal gentlemen. 'Join that queue,' he said. 'They always know the best places to eat.' Sure enough, men from the nearby law-courts were already lining up, so I joined them and have returned to the same shop ever since.

With a T.V. crew in tow, however, there was no time for even a piece of pie. It was getting late. We had been filming almost non-stop since 10.30am and it was now rapidly approaching 7pm. I was feeling quite exhausted with the effort of intense concentration, but quickly rallied when I realised that I was going to be able to drool over Daniel's original indenture again. First we did some filming in the Wills Room, where I churned away at a microfilm reader looking at the probate document of 'Daniel Bacheler, gentleman ... of Leigh'. 'Good heavens!' said Antonia, as she surveyed the room full of people, all noisily churning away at *their* readers, 'They look like battery hens. I've never seen anything like it!'

Eventually we made our way to the Round Room where Daniel's indenture, Uncle Thomas Cardell's will and Elizabeth I's Account Books were all waiting for me on the large central table. 'Now, Anne,' said Antonia, 'Do you think you can make these dull old documents interesting?' *Dull?* They were wonderful. Here was the very document my little musician had touched and signed when he was around fourteen years hold. Here was old Uncle Thomas's will, in which he called Daniel, 'my loving nephew and friend'. Here was the royal account book recording the payment of £10 to Daniel for carrying letters from Queen Elizabeth to Robert Devereux in 1599. Hardly dull old documents. Even though I was now struggling to keep my eyes in focus, and it was an effort to remember what I was doing there, once I held the indenture all my weariness lifted as if by magic.

I have studied that document many times and always feel a thrill at touching something my Daniel has touched. Some time ago, when I was going home from such a visit, the Leeds taxi driver who picked me up at the coach station asked where I had been and what I had been doing. When I told him about the indenture and tried to explain how I felt about it, he said, 'Oh, I see. You've been putting your hands on history.' I could not have put it better myself. Now, before the T.V. camera, I could perhaps share that feeling of delight and wonder with the viewers.

After this extremely long day's work I was told to be bright and early the next morning for our journey into Buckinghamshire. 'Early' I could manage, but 'bright' was going to be a problem. I am not really a morning person, as my ex-pupils know. It was an affectionate joke within my class that 'Miss Batchelor comes to school at 8.30 but never wakes up until 11!' They swore that I drove to school on automatic pilot. It was with a great deal of effort, then, that I rose early the next morning to meet Antonia.

First we drove to Chesham, a far cry from crowded Oxford Street and the claustrophobic London Underground. At the beautiful church of St. Mary, George Piggin, my 'cheerful churchwarden of Chesham', met us. He greeted me with a beaming face. 'Who would have thought that your research would have led to this?' he remarked as the camera was set up. Then he was filmed, several times, bringing the original register from its safe and showing me the marriage entry of John Bachilor and Margaret Lovett in 1580. His wife, Mary, who looks after me so well on my visits to Chesham, watched his T.V. debut with great pride. Everyone remarked on how calm and professional he looked in the finished film. I was so pleased to be able to share this part of my adventure with these good friends.

Later that morning my friend, Mary Geary, met us at Chapel Farm and was introduced to the crew. Antonia enthused over the beautiful farmhouse which has developed, over the centuries, from what was undoubtedly a more modest building in Andrew Batcheler's time, in the rein of Henry VIII. Pat filmed several takes of Mary and me driving up to the door of the house, sometimes with poor Bill, the sound man, huddled on the floor of the car so as to be out of sight of the camera.

The we went indoors, where Joan and Leslie Allen patiently put up with the film crew cluttering up their lovely home with cables and lights and camera. Joan was to be shown greeting us at the door and leading us through the first room, pointing out the wattle and daub wall, before showing us the oldest part of the house where a massive beam runs from the ground to the roof, supporting the entire structure of the house. This was the part of the house Andrew Bacheler would have known. I was very impressed at how well Mrs. Allen coped with the repeated takes demanded of her. In all she had to do her sequence *eight* times because of problems with the lights or the sound, and yet she managed to remain calm and unflustered. Mr. Allen wisely kept out of the way, dealing with the vital business of arranging lunch for us at the local pub.

After a fine lunch we left chapel Farm, which is now known as Buckland Grange. I always find this a wrench, for I feel so much at home there. We now moved on to Aylesbury, to film at the

Buckinghamshire County Record Office. Here I was given a very warm welcome by the staff, many of whom have developed a personal interest in my research over the past few years. Here I was allowed to enthuse over a heap of old wills, including those of Andrew and Joan of Chapel Farm. I still get excited when the staff give me a box of mouldering documents to study. Like a child at Christmas, I can't wait to get the box open and see the goodies inside.

The excitement of filming had kept the adrenalin going but now I had a few days off (remission for good behaviour, perhaps? to gather my wits for the last couple of days filming in Kent. I was looking forward very much to this, for I would be revisiting the churchyard where my Daniel is buried. We arrived at Lee in the early morning and filmed first at the Manor

House Library, where the original burial register for St. Margaret's church shows the details of Daniel's burial. Then it was up the hill to the churchyard where he lies in an unmarked grave. I found it very moving to bring these visitors to Daniel's last resting place, for the members of the crew had, over the last few weeks, retraced with me my journey of discovery and they all knew Daniel's story well. With great sensitivity, Pat filmed me from a discreet distance as I had a private moment with my thoughts, before placing another red rose, this time provided by the B.B.C., on one of the tombs. It was good to feel that Daniel was being honoured at last with some public recognition.

The next day we were off to Penshurst Place, the ancestral home of the Sidney family, for the final day's filming. We were welcomed by Viscount De L'Isle,

With Antonia and Lord De L'Isle, admiring Sir Philip Sidney's helmet.

descendant of the Sidney family and the owner of Penshurst Place. We entered the Great Hall, where no doubt Daniel's music had been played centuries ago. Daniel had dedicated a piece of his consort music to the Lady Frances Sidney, the widow of Sir Philip and the lady who was going to be instrumental, in later years, in furthering his career. On an enormous table, sixteen feet long, was the treasure I had come to Penshurst to see.

It was the 38-feet-long funeral roll of Sir Philip Sidney, a series of engravings showing a dignified procession of courtiers and councilmen, grieving family and friends. There was the picture of the coffin, preceded by a man bearing Sidney's porcupine-crested helmet. The actual helmet was there on the table before me. The poor porcupine had lost most of his quills now, but it was still wonderful to see an item which had been in the original procession. Following a banner in the procession were two lads on horseback. The first was little Henry Danvers, whom I had found in the account or Robert Devereux's ill-fated expedition to Ireland. When the Earl came back to England in 1599 he was 'accompanied by Sir Henry Danvers who was not yet recovered from a desperate wound he had received'. Henry had risen to the rank of Lieutenant General and was twice wounded. The 'desperate wound' was described by Sir John Harington as 'a shott in the face, the bullett passinge to the roote of his lefte eare'. Poor little Henry. As he rode in style through the streets of London that day in 1587, he little knew what lay ahead of him.

Behind Henry Danvers came my Daniel. To see this original picture of him was a thrilling moment for me. Viscount De L'Isle assured me that the portraits in the engraving are believed to be true likenesses. I was pleased about that, for when I had seen the pictures of the funeral procession of Queen Elizabeth in the Department of Manuscripts at the British Museum, I had noticed that almost all the men in the pictures had the same face. They all looked like Guy Fawkes, with narrow faces and dark, pointed beards. I imagine they were rent-a-sob mourners, ordered by the artist by the yard.

The only exception, which I found quite touching, was the figure of Robert Cecil, the Earl of Salisbury. I have a soft spot for him, since his gift of a cup to Anne of Denmark was the reason for Daniel writing his letter of thanks on behalf of the Queen. This, as you may remember, was my first discovery of a reference to Daniel. In the picture, Cecil had originally been portrayed 'à la Guy Fawkes' like everyone else, but someone must have pointed out to the artist that he had a small, misshapen body, for the original figure had been painted out with white paint. It had then been replaced by a careful representation of the twisted body of the little Earl.

The Sidney funeral roll, however, is considered to be an accurate document. It is said that named individuals in the procession match up exactly with known potraits of them elsewhere. This is the only known potrait of my Daniel, so it is good to know that it is a true likeness. Having enthused about how fine Daniel looked on the war-horse, we now adjourned for lunch.

It was at this point that I noticed a most beautiful portrait of the Lady Frances Sidney, née Walsingham, with her little Elizabeth, daughter of Sir Philip. It was wonderful to look on the face of the lady who had been such an important influence on Daniel's life. She was herself a most remarkable lady who managed to survive an extremely dangerous situation when married to her second husband, Robert Devereux, Earl of Essex. He was an unstable character described as, 'shifting from sorrow and repentance to rage and rebellion so suddenly as to prove him devoide of goode reason or right mynde'. He tried to seize power in a foolish and ill-fated attack on the palace and ended his life on Tower Green at the hands of the headsman. The Lady Frances lived quietly with her mother and eventually married for the third time. I do hope that she lived happily ever after. It was so good to see her here, sharing my *Timewatch* adventure with me.

After lunch the crew started to set up their gear in the

Long Gallery, where Jakob Lindberg, the talented young lutenist, was already warming up his fingers and his lute. It was bitterly cold, for that part of Penshurst Place is not heated in the winter. Jakob was, in fact, brewing up a nasty case of 'flu, yet in spite of his temperature and blue fingernails his playing was superb. As the lighting technicians worked to get everything just right, I took this opportunity to look around the Gallery. There I saw a likeness of Queen Elizabeth in the form of a mask. This tough lady, with her sharp features and equally sharp tongue, once danced to the music of Uncle Thomas Cardell and, quite possibly, to some of Daniel's early music, too.

At last everything was set to the satisfaction of Pat on camera, Bill with his sound equipment and the lighting engineers. This was to be a sequence in which Bill came into his own, for Jakob was going to give a recital of Daniel's music to an audience of two, the descendants of the Sidney and Batchelor families. First the 80-year-old Viscount and I had to be filmed entering the Gallery. It took six takes to satisfy Antonia, who is a great perfectionist. 'That was absolutely lovely,' she would say, 'but we'll just do it again, and this time …'

As I look now at that sequence, as we walk the length of the Gallery, I am reminded of the words of Joyce Grenfell's song, 'Stately as a galleon I sail across the floor …'. Viscount De L'Isle was quite uncomplaining as we did take after take, but I think that, like me, he was relieved when we were allowed to reach the two comfortable chairs at the far end of the room.

Then I had the great delight of just sitting there as Jakob played Daniel's *Mounsiers Almaine* over and over again. This time I didn't care how many takes it took. I could have sat there all day and watched Jakob's fingers fly across the lute. The instrument he played was a seven-course Renaissance lute and the resulting soundtrack is something I shall treasure always.

Probably the most rewarding part of this day's filming was between takes, when Jakob and I enthused together about Daniel's music. We formed an instant Daniel Appreciation Society, and only shut up when the camera was turning again. It is a great pity that my film was limited to less than half an hour, for had there been film time to spare the sight of the two of us, grinning and chattering and gesticulating wildly, would have made vibrant television. My fear was that the cool approach that Antonia wanted me to use would come across as dull and flat. However, many people who saw the film remarked on my enthusiasm, so it must have come through in spite of my being 'laid-back' as requested.

Suddenly it was all over. This was the last day of filming and I had to say my farewells to my super crew. They had been wonderfully patient and encouraging, and such fun to be with. They turned what could have been a nerve-racking and daunting experience into a real delight. In gratitude I gave them each a packet of Yorkshire Tea, to remind them of that first breakfast at my flat, and a tape of Daniel's music to remind them of the last day at Penshurst. Then it was hugs all round. As the equipment was cleared away, I heard several folk humming or whistling *Mounsiers Almaine*. I think Daniel would have been pleased. I know that I was.

Now it only remained for me to visit a B.B.C. sound

studio to record the voice-over and we were home and dry. I was shut in an airless, dark studio, with my script before me in a pool of light. Beside me was a coloured light which indicated when I was to speak. Surprisingly, I found that the most difficult thing to do was to control my breathing. I would take a deep breath, ready to speak as soon as my light flashed, but then there would be a delay while Antonia spoke to the sound technician in the next room. I would relax and breathe out only to see my light flash as soon as my lungs were empty. I knew that we were working to a very fine timing, to match the commentary with the pictures on the screen before me, so even a few seconds spent breathing in or out at the wrong moment could ruin everything.

Eventually I managed to get myself sorted out and we finished the soundtrack to everyone's satisfaction. It was not an experience that I would like to repeat too often. I felt like one of Pavlov's dogs. When my light flashed I felt I should bark or salivate! However, the various parts of the film were now ready to be put together and my adventure before the T.V. camera was over. It felt very strange saying, 'Goodbye', to Antonia. She had become so involved with my story and we had spent so much time in each other's company that I felt we were not producer and star, but friends. All the exciting things which have happened to me since *Timewatch* I owe to her first recognition of my story's potential and her vision of the programme it could become.

On the night of transmission I had a small gathering of family and friends at my flat, including Audrey, my taxi lady. My parents were thrilled at the programme and my father remarked, 'It's nice to see you making something of your life.' I was very touched. As the programme ended the telephone began to ring. It was to go on ringing for weeks, bringing me congratulations and requests for help from total strangers all over the country. One gentleman, quite unknown to me, rang from a distant county to congratulate me. When I asked how he had managed to find me, he said, 'My dear, I'm a genealogist. I'm used to tracking people down.'

Duggie, too, was kept busy as the letters started to pour through my letter-box. There were over three hundred, to all of which I replied by hand. I had intended to photocopy a standard Thank You letter, but every one of them had to have an individual reply, for a great number, besides containing congratulations, asked for help in finding lost ancestors or advice on how to start family research. Many of them contained extremely kind remarks such as, 'The most interesting piece of television I have seen for some time,' or, 'Simply marvellous — truly, what a delight!' I think the B.B.C. were surprised at the response, too, for I believe they regarded genealogy as a minority interest. Our audience for the programme was an amazing 2.4 million and the reaction index was 82 out of 100. I don't know exactly what that means, but 82% sounds pretty good to me. I was particularly touched to receive very kind letters from the crew, including a plea from Bill, 'When you make your next film, please may we be the crew?'

Among those who contacted me through the B.B.C. was an elderly gentleman in Berkshire. He asked them for my address because, he said, 'I have a coin which came from Chapel Farm and I think Anne Batchelor should have it, if she would like it.' It appears that he lived in Chapel Farm before the present owners, and, when restoration work was being done on a wattle and daub wall in one of the bedrooms, he found the coin embedded in the base of the wall. This treasure he now sent to me. It was a most beautiful Elizabethan silver sixpence, clearly dated 1584. Along with it came a charming letter in which he said he felt that the coin had now 'come home'. He signed the letter, 'J. Devereux Colebourn'. How very strange. It was as if my ancestors, across four centuries, had sent me something tangible from our farmhouse — and at the hands of a Devereux. Remember how important Robert Devereux, Earl of Essex, had been in Daniel's story? What a curious coincidence. Perhaps the ancestors have forgiven me, at last, for being so

My Elizabethan sixpence from Chapel Farm, 1584.

inquisitive about them. Incidentally, the room where the coin was found is known as the Ghost Room. Perhaps one of my long-dead Batchelors is refusing to sleep easy until he finds his lost sixpence!

Other post-*Timewatch* letters which pleased me came from people who had helped me in my original research, long before I became involved with the B.B.C. I heard from Jack Reynolds at North Church, Wilf and Ethel at Rickmansworth, the Piggins at Chesham and the staff at the Herts. and Bucks. Record Offices. What has surprised me so much about the whole *Timewatch* experience is the obvious pleasure my research has given to other people. Family research is, by its very nature, a private and personal occupation. It has been such fun for me, and it is lovely to think that it has also given a great deal of enjoyment to so many.

A gentleman who recognised me as I was researching

in the Soc. Gen. recently actually asked for my autograph. Fame at last! He went on to say, 'How wonderful for *one of us* to have some recognition at last, instead of the professional academics getting all the attention.' He was right. It *is* a nice feeling to know that, as a self-taught amateur, I have done some valuable research. So often family historians work with great dedication for years with little more than a lame, 'Oh, that's nice,' from family and friends who tolerate their passion for the ancestors as a simple-minded eccentricity. I felt that my *Timewatch* experience justified all those years spent among dusty archives, chasing my elusive ancestors. It was like a pat on the back and a 'Well done!' from the media.

I had hoped that I would find many Batchelors related to my family as a result of my film, but there was only one. I had a letter from a lady in Dorset who proved to be my grandfather's grand-niece. Her grandfather, Joseph, named after Joseph the gardener of Berkhamsted, was the brother of my grandfather, John. I had not even known that she existed, so it was lovely to meet her. I spent a happy time with Joyce, swapping Batchelor stories. Later she visited York, where I showed her the streets where her grandfather lived as a boy. Then I took her to the old cemetery to visit the graves of George and Eliza, her — and my — great-grandparents. Of course, we remembered to visit old Theophilus, too.

Among the numerous letters Duggie dropped through my letter-box immediately after my programme, there were two which confirmed my star status. The first was addressed thus:

'GPO — Please try to trace —
Anne Batchelor
who appeared in TV *Timewatch* and
lives in a block of flats in
Leeds
Yorks.'

The second came, minus stamp, from London and was addressed to:

'The lady who appeared on the B.B.C.2.
TV programme "Timewatch" on Wednesday
3 May re. Daniel Bachelor'

Congratulations to the Post Office. Someone there must have been watching my programme.

That second letter was from a delightful lady called Maggie, who began it with the words, 'Hi there!' She went on to explain that she caught the programme part way through and had no idea where I lived or how to address me. What she wanted to tell me was that she regularly caught a bus from outside the old churchyard of St. Margaret's, Lee, and had often sat on the wall wondering who was buried there. Now that she knows about Daniel she has promised to call there whenever she visits Lee so that he is not forgotten. I found that very touching. Daniel seems to have caught the imagination of so many people.

Another very satisfying outcome of the *Timewatch* film has been the increased interest in Daniel's music. I was invited to tell his story to a group of music students at Hull University, home of the Walsingham Consort Books, and at the Norvis Summer School of Early Music at Durham University. On both occasions I took my own personal lutenist, Martin, with me to play some of Daniel's music. I was invited to read a paper on my Daniel to the Lute Society, which was great honour, for Daniel as well as for me. At last he is receiving the recognition he deserves.

When I took my early retirement at the end of 1987 I told my class that I wanted to write a book about my search for my ancestors. 'One day, when I'm rich and famous,' I said, 'you will see me being interviewed on television, and you'll say you knew me when I was just a teacher.' It was meant to be a joke. I never thought it would actually happen. I met two of my ex-pupils shortly after *Timewatch*. 'Saw you on the telly, Miss Batchelor,' said Lisa. 'Yes,' said Debra with great awe in her voice, 'Saw you go into *Virgin Records!*' I don't think they thought much of the rest of the story, but Virgin Records was obviously something else. They were most impressed.

As the interest in my research continues undiminished, I have more requests for speaking appointments than I can really cope with. My father has stopped saying, 'But what is it for?' Now he understands what a thrilling, special experience my research has been. As for my mother, bless her, she is patiently waiting for me to find time to do some more research on *her* family. She, too, is pleased at the way my story has been received. 'Just think', she said one day, shortly before *A Batchelor's Delight* was shown, 'You'll be famous. You'll be in the *Radio Times!*'

From the Walsingham Consort Books.

Chapter Six

Odd Bods and Pebbles

'I don't know whose ancestors they *were* —'
W. S. Gilbert.

Any family historian will tell you that, in the search for their family, they often trawl in odd individuals who are of the right name and in the correct area, but who do not appear to belong anywhere on the family tree. These individuals I call my 'odd bods' and I have been avidly collecting them over the years, in the hope that one day their place in my genealogical jigsaw will become apparent.

My lovely lutenist, Daniel, was himself an odd bod when I first found the reference to him and his letter to Robert Cecil. There was no way in which I could have known, at that time, what an important member of my family he would prove to be, or what a difference his discovery would make to my life. What a good thing I didn't reject him but noted the reference to his letter in my little notebook. I now have quite a fine collection of odd bods. People like Thomas Batchelor of Hempstead, who was hauled before the magistrates in 1683/4 for 'swearing six oaths and abusing the watch'. He sounds awkward enough to be one of my Batchelors — but who knows?

Some of my odd bods don't even carry the Batchelor name, but I have come across them on my travels and have been amused or mystified by their names or stories. For instance, what possessed Thomas Holroyd, manager of the Gas Works at Castleford in 1881, to call his second son, Joe? After all, his other children were Zerah, Zeuriah, Zelha, Ziha, Zillah and Zibiah! Can you imagine the poor census enumerator knocking at the door of *that* house? And what confusion there must have been when he visited the family whose surname was Guess. My heart bleeds for the poor census man who scribbled in his book, in obvious

frustration: 'I can only say that from the low character of the district and the difficulties arising from it, I have done my best to make it correct.'

The enumerator's lot was certainly not a happy one. Eve McLaughlin, of the Buckinghamshire Family History Society, writes on this subject: 'Ancestors in huge numbers died, emigrated or went into hiding in the early days of March 1851 so as to avoid revealing their place of birth in the 1851 census. Those who stayed to brave it out apparently threatened the enumerator with dogs, shotguns or the bubonic plague so that he stayed outside the door, listed the children by initials only and got the ages wrong.' She could be right.

I learnt early in my research to take information on official documents with a very large pinch of salt. They are not infallible. Approximate ages given to the census man, such as, 'Grandad's about eighty,' were written down as exact. In fact the old boy could have been 77 or a well-preserved 85. What was recorded as place of birth was often the place where the person grew up and from which their earliest memories came. Their actual birthplace could be 50 miles away, or more. People lied about their first child's age to conceal a pre-marital birth, or about their own age if they feared being considered too old to be given work. Church registers, copied up every few months from hastily scribbled notes on scraps of paper in a vestry drawer, can contain glaring errors. Published transcripts of parish registers can contain serious omissions. The transcript of the Aston Clinton registers missed out my Daniel's baptism, though it is clearly listed in the original register. Even modern copies of birth, marriage or death certificates from the G.R.O. at St. Catherine's House, London, have been found to contain errors. No wonder the poor family historian feels quite desperate with frustration at times.

Even so, through the records come the stories of individual families which touch us across the years. Poor Mrs. Giggle of Horbury, in West Yorkshire, in the space of a few months lost her little Gertie Giggle, then young Nathan, along with Herbert (aged nine months) and Rufus (aged eight weeks). She had little to giggle about, poor soul. In Ossett lived a girl with the grand name of Anastasia Galilee. She was a rag sorter at the mill. Nothing grand about her life — except her name.

I cannot resist collecting the odd names I come across as I look for my Batchelors. There was Marfity Snipt, who worked in the scullery of the Earl of Dorset. She sounds as though she has strayed from the pages of a Dickens novel. Then there was Rowland Rubbish, violinist to Elizabeth I. I imagine him asking her, 'What did you think of my music, your Majesty?' to which Elizabeth replies, 'It was rubbish, Rubbish!' Probably Ann Godbless, a poor child of Westminster, was a foundling. What about Mr. Coo of St. Dunstan in the West? Did he keep pigeons, I wonder, or is he just a badly written Mr. Coe?

I wonder about the origin of Firebrace Cremer's name. I found her in the register of Swanbourne, Bucks., getting married in 1806. Then there was Plesent Emma Flint, married at St. Pancras in 1902. When John Bachelor married Love Lee at Amersham in 1795, did he tell his friends, 'My bride is a love-lee girl'? Perhaps my favourite Batchelor name is borne by Faint-not Bachelor, who married at Lewes in 1614. So the list goes on — Dulcibella Melles married Onysiphorus Hands — I wonder whose ancestors they are. You can see how easily one's attention can wander from the family research in hand. Historical records make such fascinating reading.

But back to my Batchelors. Soon after the *Timewatch* film was shown I had a telephone call from a lady who told me that, on the wall of the census office in London, she had seen a blow-up of the 1851 census for Buckingham Palace. Did I know, she asked, that a Thomas Batchelor was page to the Queen? She said that she thought it would be awful if 'that poor lady in Leeds' was searching for Thomas in Herts. when all the time he was in London. I sent for a copy of the entry and, right enough, there he was: 'Thomas Batchelor —

Married — Aged 65 — Page to the Queen.' Rather old to be a page, I would have thought. I always imagine a page to be a little lad. Sadly, his place of birth was given as Grandborough, Warwick, so he is not likely to be one of mine, but you never know.

I had already found another Thomas who was, for many years, valet to the Duke of York and Page of the Backstairs to George IV. In 1829 he was the King's Valet de Chambre and it was later written of him that 'this man Bachelor had become a great favourite with the late King'. Intriguing, but he might be nothing to do with my family, though the Batchelors often seem to have been in service to the nobility, as my Daniel was.

A Richard Bachelor, servant to the Earl of Dorset, was granted 'ground or garden plot and separate nook or angle of ground lately taken forth of the Earl's close of pasture called Covent Garden'. That would be worth a pretty penny today. Another Batchelor, John, was servant to the French Ambassador in 1617. A certain John Hall had been accused of stealing iron and other things from a forge in the Ambassador's garden. John was one of those called to give evidence against him. In the same year a Thomas Bachelor of St. Giles in the Fields, yeoman, was involved in a case against a man called Fynne, the outcome of which was that 'Fynne shall not hereafter lodge within his house a frenchman being vehementlie suspected to live incontinentlie with his, the said Fynne's wife'. All fascinating stuff, but as yet they are unconnected odd bods. My notebooks are crammed with such bits and pieces.

Who, I wonder, was Alice Bacheler of Hampton, who died in 1678? Sylvester Baldwin of Aston Clinton, my Daniel's home village, left money to an Alice Bacheler of London, and Daniel had a sister called Alice. However, if this is his sister who followed him to London, then she would have been over 100 when she died. Not very likely, though not impossible. People in the royal household were often long lived. At St. Margaret's, Westminster, I found memorials to Lady Dorothee Stafford, servant to Elizabeth I, who was 78 when she died, and Blanche Parry, keeper of

Elizabeth's jewels and Gentlewoman of the Bedchamber, who died at 82. Then I found the memorial to Cornelius Vandun who died in 1577, having been Yeoman of the Guard and Usher to King Henry, King Edward, Queen Mary and Queen Elizabeth. He built 20 houses for poor widows, at his own expense, and died at the ripe old age of 94.

In North Church, Herts., they lived even longer, if the church register is to be believed. There I found this amazing entry:

'Mother Clyfford born in the time of King Henry VII being 105 years old and more died Oct 1 1610'

I love the vague, 'and more'. She must have been quite a lady. So much for those who say, 'Of course, people didn't live so long in those days'.

The Rev. Stephen Bachiler was sent to me by an American lady. He was born in 1561 and died at the age of 99, having lived an extremely eventful life and worn out four wives. He married Ann Bates in Hampshire when he was 27. When she died he married, at the age of 62, a widow, Christian Weare. She lasted only four years, whereupon he married his third wife, Helena. She was described as 'a lusty and comely woman', a suitable partner for our sprightly 66-year-old Stephen.

At the age when most of our ancestors had retreated to a seat in the chimney corner, Rev. Stephen (aged 71) emigrated to America, where Helena died ten years later. Determined not to remain unmarried, Rev. Stephen married his fourth wife when he was 86. She was hardly the kind of wife one would think suitable for a minister. She was a widow who had been branded with an 'A' for 'beeing adulteres with George Rogers'. Perhaps she was a reformed character when Rev. Stephen married her. He appears to have returned to London in his old age and died at Hackney in 1660. What a character.

I would love to claim him for my family but there are only two slight possibilities which might draw him towards my family tree. It is believed that he was born in the Alsace-Lorraine area. I found a copy of a letter concerning an Andrew Bachiler who was reclaiming property which he said had been taken by force by the King of Spain's men. The letter was to Robert Cecil. The property was at Armentier. I wonder —? Then I noticed that one of the places listed in Stephen's biographical sheet was Hampton. Now the lady called Cecily, wife of Daniel Bacheler, who died in 1611 and who I believe could have been the wife of *my* Daniel Bacheler, was described as 'Cecily Bacheler of Hampton'. Perhaps one day I shall be able to claim the Rev. Stephen as one of the more eccentric and colourful members of my family. I do hope so, for I have a great deal of admiration for the old boy.

Coming nearer to our own time, I have several unplaced odd bods who just might belong in my genealogical jigsaw. There is dear Old Batch of Tring, yet another William. When asked what he thought about the problems in Ireland, at the beginning of this century, he replied, 'They want old Oliver Crumble back. Shoot 'em down, I say. Shoot 'em down!' His wife's scathing comment on this was, 'Yes, he says, "Shoot 'em down," and he wouldn't hurt a fly. Only yesterday he moved a frog out of the way so that the bus shouldn't run over it!' 'Yes,' said Old Batch, 'and then the little beggar turned round and laughed at me.'

They were a lovely old couple, these Tring Batchelors. Mrs. Batchelor thought it strange that the new vicar should be seen 'going about the churchyard in a Cossack'. Old Batch reckoned that one of his master's horses was so bright it could 'do anything except play the organ and teach in the Sunday School'. His wife was upset when the Vicar gave her husband a copy of Shakespeare. 'I had to take it away from him, he read it so,' she complained. When Batch's mistress asked him to clear her cabbage patch of snails, he was ready with his excuse. 'Bless you, Ma'am, they know my step. As soon as I come in the front gate, they're over that wall like a shot!' I would love to read more about Old Batch, but sadly the lady who sent him to me couldn't remember the book in which she found his story.

My friend, Mary Geary, found another strange Tring Batchelor for me, among some newspaper obituaries at the Hertford Record Office. The headlines read, 'A Curious Desire — Man who bought his own coffin', and 'Death of Eccentric Man — Wanted to be buried in garden where sister is interred'. The story concerns a John Batchelar, a well-to-do eccentric who made his fortune from the family brewery and later in the preparation of honey, the rearing of poultry and egg production. He erected at Dagnall what he called a 'Church Public House', a shelter for gentlemen of the road, where there was always ale available for the thirsty traveller. Needless to say, the shelter was often full. When the Inspector of Nuisances from Leighton Buzzard recommended its fumigation, old John was most indignant. He felt that the strong 'twist' which he sold there provided ample fumigation, though he remarked in a letter to the Inspector, 'I should, however, prefer the attendance of a pair of acolytes with incense.'

His sister, Dorcas, died ten years before John, and her body was buried in the garden of their house. Her grave was planted with beautiful flowers, and John decided that when his time came he wanted to be buried there, too. That was not his only reason for wanting to be buried there. Apparently he had a habit of sitting in his chair with one leg bent under him. This cut off the circulation and his leg had to be amputated. It was buried in the garden and John, quite reasonably, wanted to be reunited with it when he died.

In order to facilitate his burial when the time came, he bought a wicker coffin on which he pinned his epitaph:

'JOHN BATCHELAR, ESQ.
BREWER OF DAGNALL, BUCKS.
LOST HIS LEG IN THE BATTLE OF BARE, 1880.
HE USED TO MAKE THE BARRELS ROLL UP,
AND WHEN THE ALMIGHTY TAKES HIS SOUL UP,
HIS BODY WILL GO TO HELP FILL THE HOLE UP.'

He reckoned that a cheap wicker coffin was quite good enough for burial. Batchelors never like to waste money! Sadly this somewhat gruesome article rotted away before John's death. As there was no mention in his will of a garden burial, he was whisked off to the cemetery at New Mill, Tring. The Home Secretary gave permission for Dorcas to be dug up and re-interred in the same grave at Tring. Nothing was said about the lost leg. For all I know, it is still in John Batchelar's garden. I feel quite sad that his obvious wishes had not been fulfilled. As a gentleman at one of my lectures remarked, 'He must have been hopping mad!' Poor old John.

This chapter of my odd bods would not be complete without mention of my lovely Emily. It was Wilf Broughton at Rickmansworth who first came across her and mentioned her to me. She was Mary Emily Batchelor, daughter of John. He was a brewer's servant when he married Maria Gates of Chesham at Paddington and brought her to live in Church Street in 1851. Later they moved their growing family to a larger house in the High Street, near the Fotherley Almshouses. Wilf had come across Emily in the log book of the Girls' National School. She was another rugged individualist, stubborn and independent, like so many Batchelors on my family tree, including my father and myself. From the very beginning I felt in my bones that Emily was one of my Batchelors, but I am still sorting out her family tree to see where it fits into mine. Wilf was able to tell me a great deal about her early years and I have pieced together the rest of her story.

Wilf wrote, 'Emily was born in 1852 and was monitress at the Girls' National School in 1866, where she also assisted at night school. In 1868 she was apprenticed as a pupil teacher. The log book of the school records some of Emily's clashes with her over-conscientious headmistress, Martha Smith. In July 1871 Miss Smith notes: I told Emily Batchelor that I disliked to see her dress festooned over a short petticoat as she was wearing it and told her to let it down. She came this morning with it in the same style and on being told again to let it down she answered very impertinently and for some time refused to do so. I reasoned with her about the impropriety of her conduct and told her that I should expect an apology. This she refused to give and was very disrespectful in her manner. In the evening her mother came to me and tried to excuse her on the ground that I had no right to interfere with her dress. She did not intend to be impertinent but that was her manner of speaking when reprimanded. She promised, however, that it would not happen again.

'Besides teaching through the school day, Emily had to attend extra tuition from Miss Smith to prepare her for the annual examination by the inspector, both on her teaching ability and academic progress. Miss Smith did not fail to record her exasperation: Emily questioned and explained too much in reading lessons; she lost patience with the children, and in her own studies seemed unable to remember the simplest facts from one lesson to another. Emily was in further trouble with the parish clergy, who received remarks from the townsfolk on her love of dress and her walking round the town, causing remarks to be made about her.

'Lady Ebury added her admonitions and advised Emily to wear her hair in a neater fashion and wear a hat more becoming to a schoolmistress. Lady Ebury's daughter, the Hon. Victoria Grosvenor, also complained of Emily's dress and her manners in the church choir, which Her Ladyship conducted. In spite of such harassment, Emily completed her five years' apprenticeship and was presented with an attaché case as a leaving present. She won a Second Class Queen's Scholarship to Hockerill Teacher Training College, where she obtained her teaching certificate. She was appointed probationary teacher at Great Gaddesden Mixed School.

'Eventually Emily became headmistress, living alone in the school house. The school was in a sorry condition, with poor attendances and failure to earn the government grants from the "payments by results"

scheme. Emily's dealings with Miss Smith, the Rickmansworth clergy and the ladies from Moor Park, seem to have made her determined to put things right by herself. By 1882 she had an efficient school and had the respect of the vicar, the ladies from Gaddesden Place and the families of the village. It was a great surprise, therefore, to read of her resignation in that year.'

So much Wilf was able to tell me. Now it was up to me. The log book entry, in Emily's own hand, stated baldly, 'July 27th — Sent in my resignation.' Emily had thrown down the gauntlet and was daring me to discover the rest of her story. I could not ignore such a challenge. Looking again at the school log book, I noticed that a fortnight earlier she had been absent from school for two days. My imagination now got to work. Perhaps she had been ill and knew that her days were numbered? I searched the St. Catherine's index of deaths for the years 1882 and 1883, but there was no sign of a deceased Emily.

Perhaps, perish the thought, her days off had been due to morning sickness! What a shocking scandal it would be if the now highly respected Miss Batchelor was pregnant. That would certainly account for a hasty resignation. Again I spent hours combing the St. Catherine's index, now looking for a hasty marriage. How lucky we are to have the index on film at Leeds Reference Library. Researchers from other parts of the country have the nuisance of travelling to London and the reputedly highly uncomfortable experience of researching in the overcrowded St. Catherine's House.

Here all I had to do was sit in a hot, stuffy little room churning the wheel of my reader alongside five other boggle-eyed, weary researchers. The longest I have been able to endure this self-inflicted torture is two and a half hours. After that I find that my eyes run down the column of names without actually taking in what I see.

Sure enough, I found Emily, listed as Mary Emily Batchelor, marrying in the third quarter of 1882, at Camberwell, Surrey. This was well out of my area, but if she were pregnant —? I sent my money off to Stephen

Wright, a most helpful and reliable search agent, who collected the certificate from St. Catherine's for me. It would have cost me far too much to go to London myself merely for a certificate.

After a nail-biting few days, Duggie delivered my certificate. It certainly was my Emily's marriage, for there was her brother, John Joseph Batchelor, acting as witness along with Maria Batchelor. Both Emily's mother and her sister bore that name, so it could have been either of them. She was married, seven weeks after her resignation from her school, to a 27-year-old organist, Jesse Flint, who gave his address as Woodhouse Eaves, Leicestershire. As I discovered from the St. Catherine's index and the census for 1861, his place of birth was Berkhamsted, so the Woodhouse Eaves address was likely to be the one to which he was to take his bride. Emily appears to have lied about her age, giving it as 27, the same as Jesse's, when she was actually in her 31st year. You see, it is not wise even to believe the details given on official marriage certificates.

Now I was able to search St. Catherine's index for a baby born soon after the wedding. If I was right it would arrive in late 1882. Instead I found a highly respectable gap of exactly nine months before the birth of Ethel Mary Flint, born in Woodhouse Eaves in May 1883 to Mary Emily and Jesse Flint. I felt that I should apologise to Emily for having misjudged her. After little Ethel's birth the family disappeared from Woodhouse Eaves and I felt that perhaps I would never know the end of Emily's story.

However, once I have the bit between my teeth I find it difficult to let go. I wrote letters to all kinds of people in the Camberwell and Woodhouse Eaves areas, asking for help. This is what I call, 'tossing pebbles in the pool'. As a handful of pebbles thrown into a pool send ripples back, so I send a handful of letters out in the confidence that at least one will bring something back. I sent a letter to the newspaper which serves the Woodhouse Eaves area, seeking contact with anyone who knew my Flints. A cry for help to the Letters Page,

headed 'Calling all Flints — was your great-grandma a Batchelor?' brought no response at all.

I had tried this technique before, when researching my Berkhamsted Batchelors. 'Calling all Batchelors,' I wrote. 'Is there anyone there who knows my George, who married Eliza Foskett in 1861 and went to live in York?' This had brought me a lovely letter from a lady at Potten End whose grandmother was my Eliza's sister. She remembered an Uncle Jack, a railwayman from York, visiting her home when she was a girl. That was my grandfather, John. He had with him his son, Billy. 'That was me,' said my father, William. He brought with him chocolates, for his daughter worked in the chocolate factory at York. That was my Aunt Annie, who worked at Rowntrees. It was a real thrill as I read the letter to hear the bits of my genealogical jigsaw fall into place.

I took my parents to visit the lady at Potten End. Quite out of the blue, in the middle of our conversation, my father said, 'I remember that visit to Berkhamsted. There was a young girl in the family who couldn't feed herself.' 'That was my sister,' said the lady from Potten End. 'She was an invalid.' They chatted on about that visit which had taken place about 70 years earlier. All this lovely experience as a result of one letter to the local newspaper. Such is the power of the press! However, when I tried it on the problem of the missing Emily — nothing.

I flung another pebble, this time in the direction of Channel Four. They run a service on Oracle called, *Where are you now?* It was set up to help people to get in touch with missing friends or relations. As Emily was certainly missing, I decided to give it a try and sent a 'Calling All Flints' notice. I had just one reply, from a gentleman in Liverpool who told me of a Catholic priest, Monsignor William Flint. I wrote my usual plea for help, only to discover that Monsignor Flint had died in 1982. Foiled again.

Once more Emily's trail went cold, until one day during a visit to the wonderful Soc. Gen. in London when I decided to look for Jesse Flint among the books of musicians. It was a long shot, for he was probably only a humble church organist even though he called himself 'Professor of Music' on his daughter's birth certificate. There on the shelf before me, sandwiched between large, impressive volumes, was a slim book called, *Royal College of Organists, Calendar for 1922-23 and Fifty-eighth Annual Report*. Well, it was rather late in date for my Jesse Flint but it was worth a quick look.

To my delight it listed Fellows and Associates of the college much earlier than 1922. I could hardly believe my luck when I found, in the list of Associates for 1890, 'Flint, J.' An eager letter to the Royal College brought a wonderfully detailed letter from the Clerk to the College, in which he gave me details of Jesse's membership. Not only that but he gave me no fewer than *nine* addresses at which Jesse and my Emily had lived between 1883 and 1904. Together they had travelled from Woodhouse Eaves to two homes in Bexley Heath, then to Hendon where Jesse was organist of Christ Church. They had a brief spell at Jesse's home town of Berkhamsted before settling in Walsall, West Midlands. Now the hunt was up.

Almost as an afterthought the Clerk had added 'Walsall, where he held an appointment at the Girls' High School.' I could not know it at the time, but this casual remark was to lead me, through many devious routes, to the rest of Emily's story. It was another similar remark about the other Lee which had led me to Daniel's last resting place some years before. People often don't realise the great importance of their casual, throw-away remarks. I wrote to the Walsall Girls' School, asking for information on Jesse. In reply I had a polite letter saying that they were sorry but they couldn't help me. Then, as another inspired afterthought, added, 'There was a famous Miss Emma Flint, whose real name was Ethel Mary, who had been Mayor of Walsall. However, I think that there was no actual relation with the lady of whom you wrote.'

Now I could barely contain my excitement. My Emily's daughter was Ethel Mary Flint. Could she be the famous Miss Emma? I wrote to the present Mayor of Walsall, who passed my letter on to Walsall Local History Centre. They sent me photocopies of 'Miss Emma's' obituary, from the *Walsall Observer* of January 1968. She had been an absolutely remarkable woman. She was principal of Lichfield School of Art and taught art at Queen Mary's Grammar School. She was a talented artist and exhibited her work at the Royal Academy. She fought for an amazing 50 years for an Art Gallery at Walsall which was eventually built and named after her, the E. M. Flint Art Gallery. In the last war she was a group officer in the Auxiliary Fire Service.

She was a co-founder of Hydesville Towers School, where she taught history and art for a number of years when she was quite old. A statement from the school said that, 'She brought great gifts of intelligence, humanity, learning and decisiveness and placed them unreservedly at the service of the school and its pupils. Many of her old pupils remember her with affection and gratitude not unmixed with awe.' As a retired teacher myself I would like to think that my pupils remember me in the same way.

This remarkable woman became a town councillor at the age of 67 and mayor of Walsall when she was 82. When she retired from the office of mayor, Councillor Herbert Smith said of her, 'Although there had been doubts in some people's minds on whether Miss Flint could stand the pace, her courage and iron will has prevailed. She has emerged looking younger than when she set out. It is they who have tried to keep pace with her who are looking slightly haggard.' Cllr. Smith said that it was mere coincidence that during Miss Flint's mayorality the Town Clerk resigned and the Mayor's chauffeur departed to another town!

Within two years the amazing Miss Emma was dead. As I read the glowing obituary I began to feel in my bones that this had to be my Emily's daughter. She was described as tenacious and obstinate, 'a vigorous and forthright personality with an indomitable will'. This surely was the daughter of the girl who fought for her right to wear her dress festooned over a short petticoat and who wore a hat unbecoming a schoolmistress over her wild hair. I'm sure that what Emily said to Martha Smith was, 'It's *my* petticoat and I shall wear it how I please!' Miss Emma of Walsall sounded like the sort of woman who would have done the same. But where was my proof?

I tossed many pebbles into the pool, to the local newspaper, to the E. M. Flint Art Gallery and to Hydesville Towers School, but there was no joy to be had from any of them. Then came one of those moments of inspiration. Perhaps — maybe — could it be possible that Emma was buried in a family grave? Reading her obituary again, I found the name of the cemetery where she was buried. I wrote to the keeper of of records at the cemetery, telling him my problem and asking him about a family grave. Soon Duggie brought me his reply.

I opened the envelope with trembling fingers. 'It would appear,' wrote Mr. Billings, 'that Ethel Mary (Emma) Flint is, in fact, the daughter of Jesse and Mary Emily Flint, as they are all buried in the same grave.' 'Gotcha, Emily!' I crowed with delight. It was like finding a long-lost friend. The letter went on:

'GRAVE NUMBER 35-3-714
Jesse Flint aged 61 years buried 11 July 1918
Mary Emily Flint aged 80 years buried on 1 Sept. 1932
Ethel Mary Flint aged 84 years buried on 25 Jan. 1968

On inspection of the grave it was found that there is no memorial present.'

I was overjoyed. Here was my Emily's last resting place and the end of her story — or so I thought. The obstinate Emily still had a surprise up her sleeve. I asked a friend to visit the cemetery for me and put a few flowers on the grave. Knowing the exact date of burial I thought that it would be simple to obtain Emily's death certificate. Full of confidence I wrote to the Registry Office at Walsall, enclosing my cheque for £5, then I sat back to await another delivery from Duggie.

The reply came like a verbal slap in the face. 'With reference to your recent application for a death certificate in respect of Mary Emily Flint, a search has been made for the period 1930-34 without success.' I was stunned. She was buried at Walsall but didn't die there. Emily was running true to form. No sooner did I find her than she disappeared again. It was always a case of, 'Where next?' Defiant to the last, she was not going to let me have all her story without a struggle.

Wherever could she have died? Back home in Rickmansworth, perhaps, or Woodhouse Eaves, or in the schoolhouse at Great Gaddesden? Perhaps she had met Jesse there long ago, when he was organist at the village church. Perhaps he taught music to the children in her school. Perhaps — on and on ran my mind. Perhaps she wanted to return to the place where they first met? Then I pulled myself up with a start. Perhaps the Walsall cemetery records had shown where she died, as well as her place of burial. I had not thought to ask for that in my original letter, believing that they were the same. A hasty letter, explaining my predicament, to the patient Mr. Billings brought the final piece of Emily's jigsaw — or so I thought.

'It appears from the burial records that Mrs. Flint died at Carhampton in Somerset.' Now to my knowledge Emily had no relatives in Somerset, but twice before that county has cropped up in my research. I once came across a 'Mr. Batchelor of Wyrardisbury (now Wraysbury) in Bucks.' who, in 1647 'deserted his flock and went to Somerset.' I have no idea who he was but he was from my area. Perhaps he ran off with someone's wife. A touch of the Barbara Cartlands there, I think.

Later, looking through Burke's *Landed Gentry*, I came across a Colonel Vivian Bachelor who was using a coat of arms very similar to my Daniel's. He lived at Combe Florey House, near Taunton in Somerset. When I wrote to him, commenting on the coat of arms, I had a reply from a Mrs. Waugh, telling me that he had died some years ago. I had a further letter from the same address from the writer Auberon Waugh, who

Ethel Mary Flint — 'Miss Emma', mayor of Walsall, 1966.

he had died childless and the right to his arms presumably died with him.

Perhaps these Somerset Bachelors have nothing to do with Emily's visit in 1932, but it *is* a coincidence that Carhampton, where she died, is only about ten miles from Combe Florey House. It was not easy to track down the Carhampton Register of Deaths, which had been sent to Williton and then Taunton. I posted off my cheque for £5 and waited impatiently for Emily's death certificate.

At last Duggie delivered the long awaited brown envelope. It *was* my Emily, dying at Carhampton of heart disease and senile decay. Her home address is incorrectly given as Lichfield Road, when it should say Street, but she is described as 'widow of Jesse Flint, an organist'. She died at a place with the intriguing name of 'The Ramblers', and it was the occupier, C. J. Harvey, who informed the registrar of Emily's death. Perhaps the 80-year-old Emily, wearing her dress festooned over a short petticoat and with her wild hair topped by a hat unbecoming a schoolmistress, had decided to go off on her own for a rambling holiday. Did her daughter, Miss Emma, protest, only to be met by the same indomitable will as her own? I am still awaiting the explanation.

Meanwhile I was turning up a great deal more about Walsall's Miss Emma. I found the lady who had been her mayoress, who lent me some lovely photographs. Just like her mother, Emma enjoyed dressing up and 'walking around the town, causing people to make remarks about her', in her case in a mayoral procession. By following up names mentioned in her will I had some interesting telephone conversations with people who knew her. As a result one gentleman sent me Jesse Flint's own copy of *The Messiah* and one of Miss Emma's water-colour paintings.

I found an old lady in Wales who had actually lived next door to Jesse and Emily when she was a young girl. She remembered vividly the night Jesse collapsed at the church organ and was brought home, where he died the same night. She remembers my Emily as a small

kindly gave me another lead on Colonel Vivian's family. I followed this back for several generations but even the College of Arms appear to have given up their research of this family in the 18th century. It would seem that the Combe Florey Bachelors had simply claimed a slightly altered form of Daniel's arms because

Emily's birth certificate.

Marriage of my Emily to Jesse Flint.

woman, who was distraught at the sudden loss of her beloved Jesse. She said, 'Mrs. Flint was ill for a very long time afterwards.' This was a very special contact for me, for this was the only person I had ever found who had actually met my Emily. She told me that Jesse was highly thought of, and indeed his obituary tells of his skill as a composer of church music and his frequent appointments to play in fashionable London churches. It says of him: 'Of modest, retiring and unselfish nature, he endeared himself to a wide circle of friends by whom his untimely death is deeply deplored.' No wonder Emily loved him.

Other stories of Emma came in from various contacts who kindly passed me on from person to person. She was a right old battle-axe,' said one lady, 'but everyone loved her.' 'She taught boys,' said another, 'because she couldn't abide the girls.' I was told that she was the first woman in Walsall to own and ride a motorbike. That must have raised a few eyebrows. The best story of all tells how, when my Emily died in Somerset, her daughter went to collect her body. The 50-year-old Emma then brought her dead 80-year-old mother home in the sidecar of her motorbike. Trust my Emily to be unconventional to the very end. Did she come home in

73

a coffin, I wonder, or sitting up in state with the wind blowing through her wild hair? The mind boggles!

I feel sure that I have not reached the end of Emily's story yet. I wonder what link there is between old Theophilus Batchelder of York and my Emily? As I was researching her husband, Jesse Flint, a loud bell began to ring in the far back cupboards of my memory. I had a vague recollection of a Flint lodging with Theophilus in Paver Lane. I checked my very first notebook and there he was:

'*York Census 1861*
William *Flint* — lodger — married — aged 41, Occupation — Horse nail maker — born — Belper, Derbyshire.
also
Thomas Flint — lodger — age 7 — born — York'

Surely it is not a coincidence that Theophilus from Berkhamsted had a Flint lodger, when Jesse Flint also came from Berkhamsted? Perhaps old Theophilus, who was a key figure at the start of my research, will prove to be the link who will eventually confirm what I feel in my bones — that Emily really is one of my Batchelors.

I have gone into so much detail about my research of Emily, even though she is not yet a proven member of my family, for a number of reasons. First, it is a good example of how much information can be gathered when the researcher concentrates on one individual in an obsessive and persistent manner. A great deal of imagination must be used, which can be developed into what I call 'the happy art of the inspired guess'.

It shows, too, how much of family research depends on good luck, on casual remarks and bits of information which come your way unasked. If the school at Walsall had not bothered to mention the 'famous Miss Emma', if the archivist at the Walsall Local History Centre had not decided to send me Emma's obituary, if the Clerk to the Royal College of Organists had not bothered to mention Jesse's teaching appointment at the Girls' Grammar School in 1903, then I would have lost Jesse

and my Emily and their little Ethel at Woodhouse Eaves in 1883 and known no more about them. Just think what delights I would have missed.

Another important point made by Emily's story is the wandering nature of some of our people. Consider again Emily's life:

Born at Rickmansworth, Hertfordshire
Taught at the school at Gt. Gaddesden, Hertfordshire
Married at Camberwell, Surrey
Gave birth in Woodhouse Eaves, Leicestershire
Lived in Loughborough, Leicestershire
　　　　Bexley Heath, Greater London,
　　　　Hendon, Greater London,
　　　　Berkhamsted, Hertfordshire,
　　　　Walsall, West Midlands.
Died at Carhampton, Somerset
Buried at Walsall, West Midlands.

When I had searched earlier for Emily's death in the St. Catherine's index, I had actually noted the death of Mary E. Flint registered at Williton, Somerset, but had dismissed it has having nothing to do with my Emily. How wrong I was.

It is useful to remember, too, that the place of registry of a *death* is not a guarantee of the place of *burial*. Neither is the place of *registry* of a birth necessarily the actual town or village where the birth took place. Emily's daughter was born at Woodhouse Eaves but registered at Barrow upon Stoar. I would advise anyone thinking of taking up genealogy to invest in a good, large-scale road atlas. Mine is an indispensible aid to my research, helping me identify strange places such as Carhampton or Barrow upon Stoar.

Emily's story also illustrates the amount of research which can be done by post. Because of family commitments I cannot travel as freely as once I did, but my research continues. It really is quite remarkable how much ground can be covered by a few pebbles in the pool, and the number of friends that can be made through the mutual exchange of information via the post box.

I could never have gathered so much detail on the life of my Daniel without my postal contacts. Andrew Ashbee sent me lots of information on Daniel's uncle, Thomas Cardell. Adrian Cardell in Australia sent me further details of the Cardells of Cornwall, plus a fascinating reference to Uncle Thomas's daughter, Mrs. Anne Tappe, who has a memorial in the church at Freshwater, Isle of Wight. Neil Cuddy sent me, all the way from Canada, references to Daniel which he had found in court records. Lynne Hulse, an expert on patronage in Tudor and Stuart times, sent me addresses of other researchers who might be helpful. Robert Spencer sent me details of Daniel's years with the Earl of Essex and the Lady Frances.

Roland T. Baldwin, from the U.S.A., has sent me material on my Batchelors of St. Leonards, Aston Clinton, including a copy of his transcript of the Bucks. Muster Rolls for 1535 which shows my Richard Bachelor listed as 'an archer', and 'Hewe Bachylars of Chesshm Towne' as being able to provide 'a bowe' in time of war. The Baldwins and the Batchelors were neighbours in those days. I had help and encouragement from a very kind guide at Hampton Court, whom sadly I never met, the late Gerald Heath. I am in correspondence with Stephen West who is, we believe, from the family of William Gomeldon, the Groom of the Privy Chamber who shared the mysterious chest of arrows with my Daniel. The list is endless. All of these people were total strangers to me originally, but they are living proof that my pebbles in the pool technique certainly produces results.

Where do I go from here? I had promised my mother that I would spend some more time on her neglected family, my Harraps of Horbury and Dewsbury, Yorkshire, and my Godbers of Sutton-in-Ashfield, Nottinghamshire, and Castleford, Yorkshire. Then the York City Archives threw an unintentional spanner in the works. I had written to them a few weeks ago to obtain the exact wording on the burial entry of my great-grandfather, George Batchelor, for this book. In the very early days of my research I'm afraid I did not realise how vital it was to copy every word of an entry, and I had simply copied the date, name and age. Now I asked for the full entry of George Batchelor, who had died in 1906.

Because I did not give an exact date or any other details, they sent me the entry of the wrong George Batchelor. He, too, had died in 1906, but his age was given as only 36, the cause of death as 'gangrene' and his occupation as 'Sergeant, 18th Hussars'. This was certainly not my George, who was a 63-year-old stoker at the Gas Works and who died of cancer, poor soul. I have been able to discover that this other George was a Quarter Master Sergeant who had served in South Africa. He had been mentioned in despatches several times in 1901, once by Lord Roberts and twice by Lord Kitchener. I couldn't help noticing that his name was listed after W. Shakespeare! In the same year he was awarded the Distinguished Conduct Medal. A book about the history of the regiment tells how, with a group of six men, he fought and held off 40 of 'the enemy'.

Now whoever could ths gallant young Hussar be? Not the son of my George and Eliza, for their George was born in 1884. According to his age at death, the Hussar was born in 1870. Could he, perhaps, be a son of my George's brother, Charles Henry, who also came to York from the family home in Berkhamsted? His enlistment papers, which should be in the Army records held at the Public Record Office, Kew, are missing. I wonder whether the gangrene was the deadly result of a wound sustained in the South African War?

Now how on earth can I find out who my brave young Hussar really is? Perhaps if I tossed a few pebbles in the pool … Oh dear — here I go again!

Postscript

As I look around my flat at the heaps of letters and photocopies, files and scraps of paper, and as I look back over my five years of fascinating research, I am reminded of a poem sent to me by a friend. It tells of a splendid journey of discovery not unlike mine:

'When you set out for Ithaka
ask that your way be long,
full of adventure, full of instruction.
....
At many a summer dawn to enter
— with what gratitude, what joy —
ports seen for the first time;
....
to gather stores of knowledge from the learned.

Have Ithaka always in your mind.
Your arrival there is what you are destined for.
But don't in the least hurry the journey.
Better it last for years,
so that when you reach the island you are old,
rich with all that you have gained on the way,
....
So wise have you become, of such experience,
that already you'll have understood what these
    Ithakas mean.'

I think that one line above all others sums up my experience

'Ithaka gave you the splendid journey.'

Rich and famous I shall probably never be, but I have certainly had a splendid journey!

Acknowledgements

So many people have given me help with my research over the past five years that it is hard to know where to begin, but I must here record my debt of gratitude to my good friends, Mary and Ernie Geary, whose encouragement and hospitality have been absolutely essential to my research. Their friendship is a continual delight to me.

My thanks are due to the staffs at the Hertfordshire Record Office and Local Studies Library, Hertford, and the Buckinghamshire Record Office, Aylesbury. Not only did they help me, with great patience and understanding, at the start of my research, but their interest in it has continued over the years. Special thanks are due to Peter Walne, the County Archivist at Hertford, and Hugh Hanley, his opposite number at Aylesbury, for all their help and for granting me permission to use material from their archives.

I must mention here how much I owe to Antonia Benedek, producer of my *Timewatch* programme. Her faith in my story and her hard work on the project not only resulted in a superb film but also opened many doors to facilitate my research.

I am extremely grateful to Viscount De L'Isle for his hospitality when we invaded Penshurst Place to film there in 1989, and for kindly giving me permission to use the portraits of Daniel Bachiler and the Lady Frances Sidney in this book.

My thanks to Wilf Broughton of Rickmansworth for sharing his discovery of the delightful Emily Batchelor with me and for permission to quote from his article on her. Thanks, too, to George Piggin, my cheerful Churchwarden of Chesham, for all his help and enthusiasm over the years.

I am grateful to the Society of Genealogists for permission to use material from their library, and to the staff of the Public Record Office for all their expert help and advice, expecially Dr. Elizabeth Hallam-Smith.

My heartfelt thanks to my musicians, Martin

Eastwell, Jakob Lindberg and Robert Spencer, for sharing their delight in Daniel's music with me, and to Neil Cuddy in Canada for the generous way he helped me track down court references to Daniel.

The portrait of Anne of Denmark is reproduced by gracious permission of Her Majesty The Queen.

I must here acknowledge permission granted to me by the following:

J. M. & M. Armstrong for allowing me to use part of my article, 'Three Dragons for Daniel', which originally appeared in *Family Tree Magazine;*

The Office of Population Censuses and Surveys, for permission to use various certificates, the design of which is Crown Copyright and which are reproduced with the permission of the Controller of Her Majesty's Stationery Office;

Phillimore and Co. Ltd. for permission to use illustrative material from *Hilltop Villages of the Chilterns* by David and Joan Hay, which they published in 1983, and Joan Hay for giving me both her permission and encouragement to publish;

Crown Copyright material from the Public Record Office is reproduced by permission of the Controller of Her Majesty's Stationery Office;

The extract from the poem, *Ithaka*, by C. P. Cavafy translated by E. Keeley and P. Sherran from *Four Greek Poets* (Harmondsworth, Penguin, 1966) is used by permission of Rogers, Coleridge and White Ltd;

The National Portrait Gallery for permission to reproduce the portrait of Sir Francis Walsingham;

The Archivist of the Brynmor Jones Library, University of Hull, for permission to reproduce part of a page from the Walsingham Consort Books;

Eve McLaughlin for permission to use her comments on the census and parish registers;

Brian Breton of the Yorkshire Heraldry Society, for his drawing of Daniel Bachiler's coat of arms;

John Unett and David & Charles (Publishers) for the quotation from *Making a Pedigree* by John Unett;

Graham Greene and the Bodley Head Ltd. for the quotation from *A Sort of Life* by Graham Greene;

The publishers, Dent, for the phrase from *Under Milk Wood* by the late Dylan Thomas;

The Editor of the *Kent and Sussex Courier*, and Barry Boxall of the B.B.C., for permission to use their excellent photographs taken at Penshurst Place;

Woman's Weekly for permission to use their photograph on the cover of this book;

Mr. N. Potts of The Bookstack Bookshop, Berkhamsted, for the pictures from the late Percy Birchnell's book, *Bygone Berkhamsted;*

I am also grateful to the staff at Lewisham Local History Centre for their help in my research of Daniel's burial at Lee, and to the extremely helpful staff at Seacroft Library, Leeds.

My thanks to my friend, Pat Webb, for the use of her photograph of the coin from Chapel Farm.

Finally I want to record my thanks to Audrey Gibb of Regal Taxis, Leeds, and Duggie Reed of the Post Office, for the part they have played in my adventure, and my dear parents and friends, who have patiently put up with my obsessive enthusiasm — and even shared it!

Bibliography

Useful books for beginners

J. COLE & M. ARMSTRONG, *Tracing Your Family Tree*. (Family Tree Publication 1990)

S. COLWELL, *The Family History Book* (Phaidon Press 1980)

D. IREDALE, *Discovering Your Family Tree*. (Shire Publications Ltd. 1970)

L. G. PINE, *Trace Your Ancestors* (Evans Bros. Ltd. 1953)

J. UNETT, *Making a Pedigree* (David & Charles 1961)

General reference books

J. GIBSON *Genealogical Guides* — various titles. (Federation of Family History Societies 1989.)[Invaluable in tracking down elusive records at very little cost. Worth every penny!]

E. HIGGS, *Making Sense of the Census* (H.M.S.O. 1989)

C. R. HUMPHREY-SMITH (Ed.), *Atlas and Index of Parish Registers* (Phillimore 1984)

E. McLAUGHLIN *Genealogical Guides* — various titles. (Federation of Family History Societies) [Good basic information and advice, especially helpful for beginners — cheap and cheerful!]

F. C. MARKWELL & P. SAUL, *The Family Historian's Enquire Within* (Federation of Family History Societies 1985)

J. RICHARDSON, *The Local Historian's Encyclopedia* (Historical Publications Ltd. 1974)

More specialised books which I have found helpful

S. BOURNE, *Ten London Repositories* (Published by the author 1985) [I never go to London without it. Within one cover all the major record offices and genealogical libraries are listed, with such valuable information as the days they are *not* open, whether you can buy a cup of coffee there and whether there is a lavatory!]

W. S. L. BUCK, *Examples of Handwriting 1550-1650* (Society of Genealogists 1965) [Very helpful in sorting out your Marthas from your Marions — not easy when written with a pitchfork dipped in soot. There are no fewer than *twenty* versions of William, a list of numbers and dates and a table of 'Confusibilia']

E. GRAY, *Cottage Life in a Hertfordshire Village* (Harpenden and District Local History Society 1977) [A most entertaining and readable first-hand account of the life of the 'ag.lab.' and village life in the 1860s and 1870s. It contains vivid descriptions of the straw plaiting industry]

A. ISON, *A Secretary Hand Alphabet* (Published by the author 1982) [A wonderful teach-yourself A.B.C. of Secretary Hand, without which I could never have read my 16th and 17th-century documents]

R. MILLWARD, *Glossary of Household, Farming and Trade Terms from Probate Inventories* (Derbyshire Record Society 1977) [Invaluable for those of us who don't know a mashfatte from a piggin, or the difference between mockadoe and lynsy wulsy]

E. C. WILLIAMS, *Anne of Denmark* (Longman 1970) [An interesting biography of the Queen in whose court my Daniel served as a Groom of the Privy Chamber]